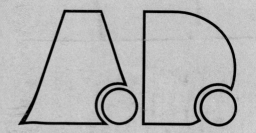

ARCHITECTURAL DESIGN
Vol 65 No 3/4 March-April 1995

EDITORIAL OFFICES:
42 LEINSTER GARDENS, LONDON W2 3AN
TEL: 071-402 2141 FAX: 071-723 9540

EDITOR: Maggie Toy
EDITORIAL TEAM: Iona Spens,
Katherine MacInnes, Stephen Watt
ART EDITOR: Andrea Bettella
CHIEF DESIGNER: Mario Bettella
DESIGN: Toby Norman, Phil Kirwin

CONSULTANTS: Catherine Cooke, Terry
Farrell, Kenneth Frampton, Charles Jencks,
Heinrich Klotz, Leon Krier, Robert Maxwell,
Demetri Porphyrios, Kenneth Powell, Colin
Rowe, Derek Walker

SUBSCRIPTION OFFICES:
UK: VCH PUBLISHERS (UK) LTD
8 WELLINGTON COURT, WELLINGTON STREET
CAMBRIDGE CB1 1HZ
TEL: (0223) 321111 FAX: (0223) 313321

USA AND CANADA: VCH PUBLISHERS INC
303 NW 12TH AVENUE DEERFIELD BEACH,
FLORIDA 33442-1788 USA
TEL: (305) 428-5566 / (800) 367-8249
FAX: (305) 428-8201

ALL OTHER COUNTRIES:
VCH VERLAGSGESELLSCHAFT MBH
BOSCHSTRASSE 12, POSTFACH 101161
69451 WEINHEIM
FEDERAL REPUBLIC OF GERMANY
TEL: 06201 606 148 FAX: 06201 606 184

D1635641

11407
FRANKS 6.4.95
£15

CONTENTS

ARCHITECTURAL DESIGN MAGAZINE

Battle McCarthy *The Power of the Brief* • *Flux Design for Change* • *Restoration and Development in* **Prague** • *Philippe* **Starck** *Interview* • **Christo** *and Jeanne Claude* **Wrapping the Reichstag** • *Lina* **Bo Bardi** • *Books* • *Highlights*

Philippe Starck, Wash basin

ARCHITECTURAL DESIGN PROFILE No 114

THE POWER OF ARCHITECTURE

Thomas A Markus *What do Buildings Have to do with Power?* • **Charles Jencks** *Aphorisms on Power* • **Erica Winterbourne** *Architecture and the Politics of Culture in Mitterrand's France* • *Franz Schulze* **Philip Johnson**: *Life and Works* • **Kim Dovey** *Place/Power* • **Mark Wigley** *Terrorising Architecture* • **Polshek** • *Heikkinen-Komonen* • **MGT** • *Pi* **De Bruijn** • *Sir* **Norman Foster** • *Santiago* **Calatrava** • *Jean* **Nouvel** *and Emmanuel* **Cattani** • *Coop Himmelb(l)au* • **Böhm** *and Steinigeweg* • *Alsop & Störmer* • **Mehrdad Yazdani** • *Dworsky* • **Rémy Butler** • *Peter Kulka* • **Stan Allen**

Ionica Building, Cambridge, computer animation still of seasonal operation conditions

Stan Allen, Demarcating Lines, Beirut, 1991

R204248

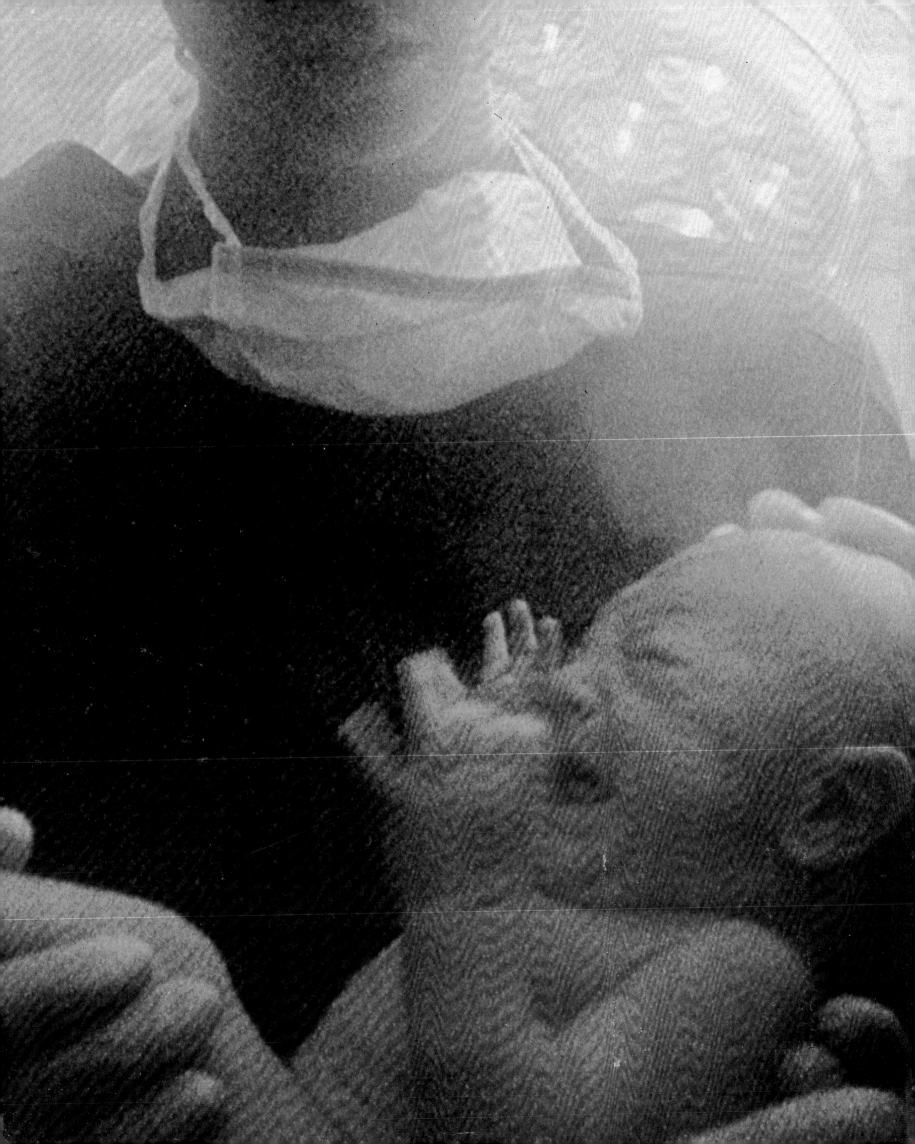

GUY BATTLE AND CHRISTOPHER McCARTHY

MULTI-SOURCE SYNTHESIS
The Power of the Brief

The primary goal of engineering is to maximise the use of materials, energy and skills for the benefit of mankind.

Before an engineer may proceed to collaborate with architects in engineering a building or new town it is imperative know what the architect is trying to achieve. Then a discussion may be initiated on how such a vision may be best engineered with available resources.

Too often, designers launch into the design process to achieve an architectural statement without the necessary research and analysis of all the issues associated with the creation of a quality brief. In particular, the brief for the internal and micro-climatic environment should consider appropriate definition of the parameters of light, sound, temperature, and air movement.

Presently, comfort is associated with extreme environmental control in terms of fixing the quantity of ventilation, humidity, light, heat and cooling to precise levels. The ultimate in comfort has been described by property agents as the tightest control which may only be achieved by sealing the building and servicing it with conditioned air. However, providing such tight control requires the installation of expensive air conditioning equipment which results in high energy demands upon our limited resources.

We are beginning to understand that the environmental brief requires much more than specification of universal rates which have little to do with the particular needs of the users or the climatic context. Our understanding of perception and comfort is lacking but we are starting to realise the complexity and unpredictablity involved; as varied as are individuals and climatic zones.

What is clear is that the old idea of a homogeneously maintained environment is being seriously challenged. To the new generation of architects and engineers, the old specification for working environments – 500 lux across the working plane, air at a constant temperature of 21°C and four air changes per hour – is anathema.

This is a response to long-unheard building users, whose views are at last being sought in a market-oriented age. In a recent survey carried out for property consultants Richard Ellis, Harris

Research interviewed 480 directors and senior managers. Ninety per cent of them said they preferred a building without air conditioning, many believing that natural daylighting and effective ventilation are important design features. Air conditioning was so unpopular, in fact, that financial institutions with investments in air conditioned buildings should be seriously concerned. Why invest in costly air conditioned developments which are less valuable to the user than low cost passive engineering solutions?

This survey indicates that for the first time this century our industry is in a demand-led market. But our attempts to understand this deep and unknown realm are still in their early stages. Current methods include quantifying temperature comfort by smelling armpits to classify BO, and charting space according to the percentage of people dissatisfied (PPD). However there are new tools emerging – based on the use of computers to model the environment in three dimensions – which enable the beginning of a description of the variety and interaction between elements. The task is not to define all-inclusive solutions, for we know that this is impossible, but to explore the mystery of the interaction of natural forces. We may then be able to create spaces providing the variety of conditions that human experience demands.

Climatic Awareness

The human body is extremely sensitive to variations in light, heat, sound, touch and airborne smells, but perception varies dramatically from person to person. People will not agree unanimously on their preferred climatic condition, especially if they are foreign in a particular climate.

In northern countries, people prefer to walk on the sunny side of the street whereas southern Europeans prefer to walk on the shaded side. Religions of the Northern hemisphere are based upon the solar cycle whereas those nearer the Equator are based upon the lunar cycle. Mistral winds in southern France are not considered a problem by the locals who accept their coming as natural – as the rise and fall of the tides.

How different are the characters of the seafarer and his opposite, the inland farmer. One so responsive to challenge and eager in its pursuit,

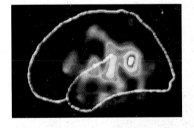

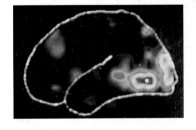

OPPOSITE: The moment of birth into our artificial environment. Photograph Pictor International; FROM ABOVE: The mystery of human behaviour; Positron Electron Tomography scan images of the brain for hearing and seeing

and the other cast in tradition and resistant to change. The different environments have created different characteristics, the different individuals dwell in different worlds.

There is no doubt that unpredictable climate makes nations more inventive in unpredictable weather. The experience of planning a barbecue at the weekend, to be spoilt by rain falling as our guests arrive makes us responsive to disappointment and induces us to seek an alternative. Does a more tempered climate influence a nation of tolerance, and a more stable and predictable climate influence a nation into becoming more organised? People living in extreme climates are focused on survival, but those in kinder climates are more at ease with the climate.

Perception also changes over time. During the summer, northern Europeans migrate to southern Europe's hotter climate in search of a more reliable sun to create their image-conscious tan, but in the last century tanning of the skin was avoided by the upper classes who associated it with labourers of the field. Nowadays weekend visitors pay a premium for views of the countryside whereupon local farmers construct buildings which look inwards, preferring to forget the outside once within. In the last century railway passengers would draw their curtains while travelling through the Alps, to avoid looking at the rocky wilderness. Now we pay a premium for views from ski chalets, and wilderness is our ultimate idea of beauty.

In buildings, we know that perception of comfort is directly related to the form and environment of the building. For example people in sealed air conditioned buildings are sensitive to minor variations in temperature and light level – leaving them very vulnerable to air conditioning system underperformance or breakdown (a major contributory factor to the association between air conditioning and sick building syndrome). But in buildings where people can open the window and experience the external climate conditions, their expectations become adjusted to the seasons, and their tolerance of variation increases dramatically. It is also clear that the influence on comfort of radiant, as opposed to convective, heat is often underestimated.

Building users' perception of the environment and climate is complex and diverse, everchanging with historical tradition, geographical location and between individuals. These variations cannot be standardised simply to make the life of property agents easier. The challenge is to give engineering and architectural interpretation to this variety.

The Art of Environmental Engineering

Environmental design is the science and art of designing and making large enclosures and building units with economy and creativity, so that they can respond to climatic forces to which they may be subjected. Our industry needs to expand upon environmental engineering practice, design development and research, education and training in association with artists of all disciplines.

How can we be creative about light, temperature, air movement and sound? More generally, how does the sense of 'naturalness', or contact with the outdoors affect people's acceptance of a varying internal environment. With the development of intelligent buildings and increasing internal climate control, how is user-control to be integrated with automatic control? There are also issues of the 'politics' of workplace control – who opens windows or regulates solar penetration, light and ventilation? What balance should there be between user comfort and management stimulation? Is there a natural aesthetic link between building form and its response to the climate and how may the designers make their operations more 'legible' to the user?

There are many more questions than answers and we must look for new relationships with art. Perhaps a greater role for artists in building design should be created in the development of the environmental brief – rather than their staid role in adding objects of art to the built form?

Architecture embraces many arenas including the art of performance. Education in our schools, including painting, sculpture, drawing and music, is fundamental training for individuals to assist the growth of their awareness of natural forces, and of how those forces may be coherently balanced within a single constructed form.

The art of environmental design is a growing market with a premium. It will not be too long before we see the rents for buildings of environmental quality and variety outstrip that of air conditioned ones. Architects need to take the lead and utilise their communications skills to inform property investors of the potentially rich returns for context-sensitive environmental design – and of the risks associated with homogenous values for comfort conditions. Our problem is that we have become so involved in product design that we are more interested in what we can build, instead of why.

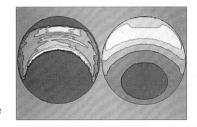

OPPOSITE: On rabante la grandevoile, par gros-temps, a bord du *Garthsnaid (photomontage);* *FROM ABOVE: The eyes of the female housefly are made up of 4,000 ommatidia, each of which sees a fragment of the world; computer modelling of daylight dispersion; measurement of the unit of smell – the Olf*

FLUX – DESIGN FOR CHANGE

The new headquarters for the telecommunications company Ionica at Cambridge forms a practical demonstration of the principles of environmental design for an ever-changing variety of human comfort expectations. Designed in close cooperation between the client, the engineers and the architect, it set out to allow variation in conditions over the day and the year while remaining within certain fixed limits. The principle is one of environmental control by structure, where the form and fabric of the building are used to manipulate the changes in prevailing conditions to create a comfortable and dynamic interior.

Cedric Price recently urged architects to become more cognisant of time – undoubtedly the quintessential modern dimension. Buckminster Fuller observed that pollution is merely a resource in the wrong place, and we are beginning to realise that a demand for heating or cooling is merely energy available *at the wrong time.*

The advent of complex but affordable iterative calculation has enabled us to translate this insight into building form. In the old days of glass curtain-walled buildings with giant air conditioning plant, engineers merely executed the calculations that were possible within their limited resources of time and calculating power – carrying out a clerical exercise to determine the size of plant necessary to cope with peak conditions in such a building. The resulting plant was oversized for most conditions and wasteful of energy; however, a static calculation was not expected to be accurate for more than a few moments of time.

The dynamic calculations now available through computers enable buildings to be designed for many different moments of time – when used to provide a useful description of behaviour on the right scale of operation (as opposed to the macro-scale of weather patterns and the micro-scale of molecular behaviour). The Ionica building is designed on the basis of a detailed understanding of how its components interact with the climate and occupants from day to day and season to season, based on complex computer analysis.

The challenge is to respond to a typical Cambridge year of weather, passing through a cycle of old winter, warm mid-season and hot summer. To ensure that the occupants do not become too warm in the summer and too cool in the winter, the structure, materials and form are used as a climatic modulator, though the principles of operation vary for each season – the main images opposite describe the principles of operation for the day and night condition in each season. The principal elements consist of ventilated standard precast hollow-core slabs, adjustable facades with shading, a central atrium and wind towers. The whole is controlled by a Building Energy Management System (BEMS) which constantly

monitors internal and external conditions, opening and closing windows and wind tower vents, adjusting the background lighting level, opening windows and operating fans where necessary. Occupants also have full local control enabling them to vary conditions at will.

The building layout consists of two daylit linear blocks oriented on an east-west axis. Cores are located at the east and west ends to block out low angle sun and overhangs provided on the southern facade control high angle summer sun while allowing for solar gain from low-angle winter sun.

During the mid-season period the building is naturally ventilated. The wind towers in combination with the thermal stack effect in the atria create cross-ventilation for the offices. In the winter, heat loss is minimised and solar gain is maximised. The heat from the top of the atria is used to preheat fresh air ducted to the offices. During the summer the cool night air is vented through the hollow core slabs so they perform as 'chilled' slabs during the heat of the day. In peak summer periods, for what is expected to be one per cent of the time, precooled air is supplied to the offices at low level where most beneficial.

Floors are precast hollow core slabs, which act as heat stores; in summer absorbing the heat of day to reject it at night, and in winter preserving the relative warmth of day against the night's cold. The atrium of the building can itself catch heat when required and uses wind and stack effects for cross-ventilation of the building in summer, bringing cooling air movement across the occupants.

The process is difficult to visualise in static images. Opposite, in the background, are stills from a computer animation created to describe the operation of the building over a day and night in early or late summer, and which proves strangely hypnotic viewing even though it is soundless; captivating and subverting normal perception like time-lapse photography of changing weather patterns. It shows the air flows through the building created by stack effect and wind suction; and the change in slab temperature through the day and night. During the day, the slab is cooler than the air, and its exposed soffit radiates coolness to the building occupants. Towards the end of the day, the slab heats up, reaching its maximum temperature in the early evening when the building's occupiers have gone home. At night, air is blown through the hollow cores absorbing heat, precooling the slab for the next summer day to come.

Ionica was designed as a moving picture, not a still. Nevertheless, it is interesting that some of its most prominent architectural features are those concerned with environmental control by structure; the wind towers, the shading devices, and form of the building itself. It is the beginning of an architecture which has thrown off stylistic preferences to create form through complex dynamic function.

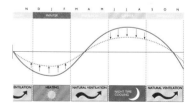

FROM ABOVE: Elevation; view of southern window with solar shading; internal view. Photographs Timothy Soar; principle of seasonal operation showing 'peak-lopping' of the energy demand curve'; OPPOSITE: Diagrams of seasonal operation conditions of the building, over stills from a computer animation created by Mark Wise

*Architect: RH Partnership, Cambridge
Environmental Control by Structure Consultants: Battle McCarthy
Service Engineers: Rybka Smith Ginsler & Battle
Structural Engineers: Hannah Reed Associates
Quantity Surveyor: Davis Langdon & Everest
Draughting & Acoustic Consultants: Cambridge Architectural Research
Wind Tunnel Studies: Bristol Aeronautical Research*

RESTORATION AND DEVELOPMENT IN PRAGUE

Prague boasts one of the best preserved historic city centres in Europe. Indeed, the Old Town has almost a fairy-tale quality. This is not primarily the work of energetic conservation committees. State subsidised conservation which was introduced in 1850 has played a positive role, but Prague's survival is chiefly due to a series of historical mishaps.

In 1935 the allies effectively sacrificed Czechoslovakia to Hitler in a misguided attempt to avert the impending war. If any benefit came from this it is that Czechoslovakia was not fought over. Prague suffered little damage during the war, the most notable exception being the last minute destruction of the rear of the town hall in Old Town Square. This was blown up by the SS in 1945 as the already defeated Germans were pulling out of the city. Czechoslovakia was then abandoned again by the West and fell under the Communist regime for the next forty odd years. Surprisingly, this also proved decisive in the preservation of the historic centre of Prague.

Under Communism the State embarked on extensive social housing projects. Its resources were channelled into developing cheap, mass produced housing largely located on the periphery of the city. The expenditure required to carry out these schemes and to provide adequate public transport to serve these new dormitory suburbs meant that very little construction work was attempted in the city centre. Notable exceptions were the construction of the metro, the construction of the Magistral Highway (which divides the National Museum from Wenceslas Square and is seen by many as State funded vandalism) and ultimately the monstrous Palac Kultury, an obscenely expensive cultural/conference facility built by the party to house State functions and known universally as 'Moby Dick'. Otherwise, construction was limited mainly to the dividing of larger residences into tiny flats for all. It could be argued that the historic centre has been artificially preserved. The reality of 'social' pressures to provide housing and the lack of 'market' pressure associated with city centre development in the West has allowed the fairy-tale core to remain relatively unscathed.

Current situation

Following the Velvet Revolution in 1989 and the end of Communism, there has been an influx of Western capital and ideals. This has been both a great threat and opportunity for the city. Prague is in a unique position. The historic centre, though desperately in need of money for maintenance and restoration purposes, is intact, and the money is now available to carry out these works. The city is also in the privileged position of having witnessed and hopefully learnt from mistakes which have been made in the development of other Western European cities.

This decisive moment for Prague's future is internationally acknowledged by those who recognise the value of retaining this unique heritage. The Cooper Union School of Architecture, under the leadership of John Hejduk (Czech Grandparents) is holding a forum to discuss issues of free-market development in the city. In 1991, 'Workshop Prague', an international ideas competition set by the Office of the Chief Architect, hoped to address these problems. However, the elegant drawings submitted by a host of well known architectural figures failed to address the key issues. One modest Czech submission in text form succinctly cut to the heart of the matter when they stated that until adequate regulation plans and clear legislation are in place the city is in danger from the very people it needs most, that is foreign investors, developers and companies wishing to establish a base in this, Europe's most central city.

Architectural layering within the city

The city has a record of confident assimilation of the new into the existing historical fabric. A tour of the castle reveals traces of the earliest settlements from the ninth century to the famous Plecnik reconstructions of the 1920s. Early Romanesque elements of the castle were both added to and in part demolished to make way for larger Gothic buildings which were in turn adapted and replaced by buildings from the Renaissance and Baroque periods. This natural accumulation of layers continued through to the 'modern' period with Plecnik's extensive reworking of the castle fabric and his design of many new elements inserted to stand in counterpoint with the preserved ruins. It is interesting to note that in Britain, however, the process of over-

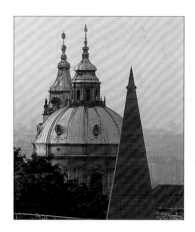

OPPOSITE: Old Town Square; FROM ABOVE: Josef Plecnik pyramid and view across Malá Strana – 'Architecture for a New Democracy' exhibition at Prague Castle 1996; Tynsky Dvur detail (photo: Radovan Bocek);'Paneláks'

layering mysteriously stopped in the past. A tentative, self-conscious attitude towards dealing with historic contexts prevails there today (note the recent winner of the competition to restore St. George's hall which was damaged in the fire at Windsor Castle).

This difference in attitude may have its roots in the inter war years. For Czechoslovakia, The First Republic (1918-35) was a time of tremendous confidence. The nation was newly independent, technically highly advanced (most of the industry of the Austro-Hungarian empire was in Bohemia) and economically very successful. At a time when the rest of Europe was under fascism or depression, Czechoslovakia was a prosperous and forward looking nation. The artistic and intellectual avant-garde flourished. This confidence found expression in the outstanding quality of modern architecture constructed in this period. This rich legacy has meant people here have no automatic antipathy towards modernism.

Commercial pressures/development control
As noted at 'Workshop Prague', the success of how the city will develop with the influx of capitalism will depend ultimately on the planning legislation already in place.

Overall an astonishing level of bureaucratic control is applied to the building process. Very few people really understand the intricacies of the development control which involves obtaining dozens of permits from up to eighty different authorities. Democracy is less intrusive than in Britain and in the Czech Republic the absolute power of informed if occasionally opinionated officials is a welcome change from the lowest common denominator input of lay planning committees (and princes).

Although permits may be needed from authorities as obscure as the Vltava River Catchment Authority, the Chimney Authority, the Military Communications, and even the Civil Aviation Authority – control of basic changes of use is still vague and unsatisfactory.

The other crucial area of control which is unfit to withstand commercial pressure is parking legislation. New office developments in the historic city centre are obliged to provide high levels of parking provision. While in the short term it is at least another factor which restricts development, in the long term it will contribute disastrously to the over use of the car.

Though the sheer density of bureaucracy is quite effective in curbing development at the moment, the system is not designed, as the British one now is, to balance commercial pressures. It will be interesting to see what happens. A lot will depend on how architects here respond to the new commercial realities and if they can responsibly reconcile the needs of their new commercial clients with broader environmental/social responsibilities.

In the summer of 1994 the travelling 'City Changes' exhibition and the accompanying symposium came to Prague. Although the lectures by a number of eminent British architects were well attended, the general message of the event as a celebration of the success of the City of London Planning Authorities was lost on most who came to look and listen. If anything was to be learnt it was that blindly following the rules of market forces destroys more than it creates. The senseless over development of the City of London in the 1980s serves as a physical reminder that such 'boomtown' short term policies are a totally unrealistic way of dealing responsibly with the growth and development of our cities.

Many Western clients seeking to establish themselves in the Czech Republic prefer to work with Western architects as this both cuts down communication problems and they are able to deliver a Western standard of service and finish which these clients expect. Currently one of the largest western architectural firms practising in

BELOW L TO R: Malé Náměstí prior to refurbishment of the Ericsson Palace; plan of Ericsson Palace before refurbishment

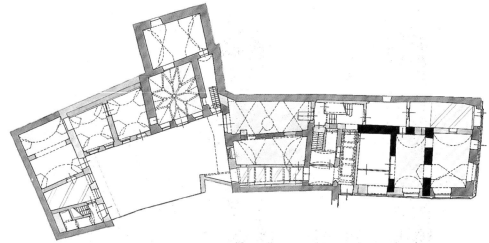

Prague is Jestico + Whiles, which established an office here in 1992, on the strength of its realisation for the offices of the British Council. The practice tries to maintain an even balance of English and local architects and has always strongly advocated the greatest use of local skills and materials. It has found much of its work involves restoring and refurbishing buildings in the heart of the historic centre of Prague which is largely a conservation area and thus entails involved discussions with the heritage department. The people in this department are predominantly historians and architects who are each responsible for an area of the city which they know intimately and they are all, on the whole, intelligent knowledgeable individuals with an interest in preserving the best of the old and to whom inclusion of well designed new elements is equally important.

Case study

One of the most interesting jobs in Prague for Jestico + Whiles was the recently completed refurbishment of the Ericsson Palace, a building located on the King's Way in Malé Námestí (Small Square). The King's Way traces the path of the coronation processions of the Bohemian Kings from the Old Town to St Vitus' Cathedral in the Castle complex. The majority of buildings which line this route are Gothic and Romanesque houses that were later rebuilt in the Baroque period. The Ericsson Palace contains elements of all these periods.

The refurbishment comprises offices, residential and retail uses. The architects wanted their additions to the building to read clearly as late 20th century elements. To achieve this it was vital to understand the different layers that already existed within the building. A document analysing the building's development was prepared by an eminent local historian prior to starting building work. It included a beautiful set of drawings which documented in detail the

seven centuries of construction in the building. The existing fabric was extensively probed and analysed and all historic items throughout the building were documented before any work began. In parts of the Ericsson Palace up to twelve layers of plaster were found, many areas revealing traces of painting from various periods. Whilst not insisting that all such finds be exposed the authorities were concerned that they should not be destroyed. It was important that plaster in the older parts of the building be 'made good' rather than replaced by new.

The building was founded in the late 12th century and its tunnel vaulted cellars are typical of this period. Although now three metres below the street, the cellars were the ground floor of the house until the streets of the Old Town were raised at the end of the 13th century as a measure against flooding. Stone window frames from this period can still be seen in the walls and the original cobbles remain on the floors.

To the rear of the house there is a small vaulted Gothic hall which was built in the 14th century for the Guild of Bakers. Experts believe the hall to be the work of Mathius Rejsek, architect of Prague's Powder Tower. The hall was the subject of a specialist restoration study and the floor level was lowered by approximately 600mm to its original level. Careful integration of the services was particularly vital in this area to prevent any damage to the historic fabric. The introduction of services, especially air conditioning into buildings such as the Ericsson Palace is one of the most difficult things to do satisfactorily. Western clients come to Prague with an expectation of acquiring a building with a level of services on a par with a speculative office block in London or New York. Providing these services requires adding a whole new layer to the building, and if not very carefully considered their installation can be enormously destructive. Service ducts run throughout and cannot respect boundaries in the way other architec-

BELOW L TO R: Exterior view of Ericsson Palace; entrance to winter garden

tural elements can. Prague's climate is more extreme than London's and air conditioning is welcome at times, but there may be a case for the planning authorities to have more powers to guard against the unnecessary insertion of services in certain cases. This is not an argument against modernising services in historic buildings, it is rather a plea to recognise that it is a difficult thing to do well. Research is needed in the field of how standardised systems can be adapted cleverly for inclusion in these buildings.

Aside from the Gothic Hall a further Gothic fragment was uncovered during construction. A small flight of stairs from the 19th century passed through a late 17th-century baroque vault in the first floor. It was proposed to demolish this stair and restore the vault. Demolition, however, revealed a fragment of a wall painting apparently dating from the early 17th century, which had remained intact behind the vault. Further investigation revealed that this painting itself concealed a valuable 14th century mural running the whole length of the vaulting. Three options were considered: removal of the wall paintings for display, retention of the 17th-century vault leaving the paintings in place after they had been investigated and recorded and finally the removal of the vault and *in situ* conservation of the painting. The latter option was chosen. The 17th-century wall painting was detached for display in the building and the 14th-century painting is now visible in its original position.

The medieval painting was a secular work which proved to be the most valuable find in Prague in the last ten years. Scholars are presently trying to unravel the story illustrated. It is known that the Italian chemist of Charles the Fourth lived in the house at this time and there is some debate as to whether the painting illustrates a Czech or Italian scene.

Construction work was rescheduled in the vicinity of the painting to avoid delay in the building process and Jestico + Whiles negotiated a grant for the costs of the conservation. The considerable co-operation between the architects and conservation officials throughout this period meant Jestico + Whiles had established a good working relationship with the authorities whereby they could negotiate more freedom when it came to inserting new elements.

In the courtyard of the building they proposed to build a winter garden to link the ground floor rooms. It was a totally new element and as such the architects felt that this should clearly be of a contemporary design. They proposed a colonnade of triangular section steel columns from which was hung a frameless glazed wall. The whole piece was readily accepted by the planning authorities despite the new vocabulary of materials being inserted into what would be classed as a grade 1 listed building in England.

Overall the practice is positive about this experience with the authorities. Discussions were generally constructive, informed and reasonable, with each side respecting the objectives and priorities of the other. Jestico + Whiles was fully aware of the responsibility of working in Prague's Old Town in a building such as the Ericsson Palace. The heritage officials for their part, recognised the connections between commercial viability in the scheme and the conservation of the building. The end result is a building which provides well serviced and efficient commercial, residential and retail accommodation, while securing the conservation of one of Prague's most valuable historic town houses.

In the broader context, if planning legislation is adapted to respond to commercial pressures particularly in the fields of 'change of use' and parking control, Prague can probably look forward to a highly successful renovation programme. The equal respect afforded to both historical scholarship and contemporary design is significant: the intelligent manner in which these issues are being handled reflects the high levels of cultural awareness and education found here, and should set an example to all the so called 'advanced' nations.

All photographs are by Pavel Štecha unless otherwise stated.

Case study: Ericsson Palace
Jestico + Whiles, Prague
Design team: Robert Collingwood,
Rachel James, Július Rybák

PHILIPPE STARCK
AN ARCHITECTURAL DESIGN *INTERVIEW*

*P*hilippe Starck is a diagnosed amnesiac. He cannot remember what he did yesterday. He cannot find his way around Paris without a map and a set of instructions as to what time he should arrive at and leave a meeting, an itinerary which his wife used to give him.

KM: Do you think that the result of your not remembering the last thing you said means that you always create new designs?

PS: I am sorry, I shall repeat just to be sure because my English is not so good. If I am known because I always produce new things?

KM: Yes, you forget the last thing you've done so you create something completely new every time.

PS: I don't know if I am known for always producing new things. I hope not, because only new things don't mean they are good things. That is why I prefer to be known to produce good things, I hope; sometimes good things because I am not perfect. But it is an important point because I think that yesterday the idea of production was to produce new things and today, I think, is really more about trying to make political action, and when it is real political action then it is a good thing, a good product. For me, trying to make beautiful things for beauty, or design for design's sake is of no interest for a lot of reasons, because, really seriously, I don't know what is beautiful and afterwards I am always very anxious with everything cultural. I prefer, more and more, to produce something which is not, I repeat, 'beautiful', but which is good. It must be of good quality but good overall – for humans, for the people who will use it. There are many ways to make a good product that can function well for people and can bring some pleasure, some love, some . . . I don't know what. That is my job.

KM: So do you think that if you are trying to produce products for people that they should be very clearly functional or do you think that is not the most important thing?

PS: It is strange that you say that, but I think I am purely functional, which suprises some people. But I am completely in line with the functionalist of the 20s, of the 30s, of the Bauhaus. The difference is that time has passed. In the 20s function was very rational in terms of weight, comfort, size, I don't know, the cost, the quality of the metal and things. That is strictly what we call the function. But today, 50 years after the vulgarisation of Freud, of La Kant, we know there is another way in which function can improve people's life. I am a functionalist, a New Functionalist; meaning that sometimes the product must be strictly functional like the Bauhaus, but sometimes the function, the main function . . . I am sorry the product must be always functional, always . . . but sometimes the function becomes less visible, sometimes there is more to offer. Take, for instance a very simple and popular thing like the lemon squeezer. There are a lot of lemon squeezers on the market. This one does not work badly but there are a lot, I am sure, that work better. The difference which contributes to the incredible sucess of this product is that it offers something else. If you have a poor kitchen because you are not rich, you can buy a product like this and it is a sort of micro-sculpture which enriches the kitchen; that is the real service for me. I love this small kind of service.

KM: And what about the Big Berta kettle which is too hot to pick up apparently?

PS: The kettle, I must tell you, is not such a perfect product, though it is not a bad product. It is not really a problem of the handle being warm because there are a lot of kettles like this – I cannot tell you . . . it is not for me. I am very proud of the toothbrush, I am very proud of the lemon squeezer, I am very proud of – I don't know what, though not very proud of the kettle. It is an old product and at the time I just tried to make the object mysterious, focusing on the idea of making this appear the entrance of the water and things like that. I am not sure today it was perhaps the main idea.

KM: Do you know of Jacques Derrida?

PS: I know nothing, I am stupid really.

KM: No you are not.

PS: Oh sure, sure, sure, sure . . .

KM: Where his philosophy has been manifested in architecture, for example, it deconstructs objects making people question the way that they use things. Are you trying to make people question how they use things?

PS: Oh definitely. I think you know everything if you ask this question. When people ask me to define myself, the only exact definition I find which is not very easy, which can look a little complicated, snobbish, is: producer of 'fertile suprise'. That means my only job is trying to propose a better life, for people to make of it what they want, and try to wake up. I think there are too many spectators and not enough actors. That is why I try – through a strange building, through a strange lemon squeezer, through a strange motorcycle, through a strange . . . I don't know what – to wake up people and say: 'Wake up, please, look how everything can be different. I just choose everything to be different. Why don't you do that yourself, with your life?' That is my job; because I don't want people to stay asleep the way they do, otherwise I don't know where we'll go.

KM: The bathroom which you have recently made using the theme of the bucket, where the loo and the sink are shaped like a bucket and the bath is like a tub – you were trying to get rid of the tap?

PS: Oh it is complicated, but for the bathroom the idea was that of trying to come back. The *salon de bain* is trying to return to the elegance, to the basic thing, to the basic materials on earth. Think of a primitive black man in the desert who wants to drink water and the way he does that, the beautiful movement – the way we move the tap is very vulgar. That is why I have tried to make this step, because it is more elegant and in danger of disappearing. I have

tried to return to the sense surrounding water, the relationships around the bucket that's all.

KM: And how does this apply to architecture?

PS: Well it is the same thing for me; whether a toothbrush or a building, it is the same thing. The main target for me, I repeat, is not for somebody walking along the street who sees one of my buildings to say, 'Oh that is a beautiful building', because there are a lot of beautiful buildings. I would prefer that he goes, 'Hah, that's strange!' and continues to walk, and while walking continues to think it is strange. This creative 'fertile suprise' . . . I am sorry it is the end of the day . . . after this suprise I hope he starts to work by himself for himself. That is why, for me, architecture is subversion. My buildings are no less comfortable than others; it is very easy to be out of the rain and cold and warm. I think we have the same quantity of sun, the same flat floor, everything the same, but there is something else to do. The urgency is for architecture to become more interesting than TV and Nintendo, because if the street and the city continue to be nothing, like today, people will continue to stay at home. When they come back in the street it will be to make Sarajevo and Beirut.

KM: How will you implement this in relation to Rue Starck, the street that you propose to design in Paris?

PS: Oh, it is exactly the same thing. I am Rue Starck, I am in the new piece of the Rue Starck, and that is moving very slowly now because it is difficult, 'oh la!' But with every building it is a different proposal. It is a Russian Salad where people will always find something to dream.

KM: Something stimulating?

PS: Exactly. Not more. I am not an architect, not a designer, I am just, oh, a 'citoen' (citizen) a member of the society – that means somebody responsible who works with and for society.

LEFT TO RIGHT: Bath, wall hung WC and bidet from Philippe Starck salon de bain, C P Hart's showroom, London

KM: Situationist?

PS: No, no, no, 'citoen' everybody is a 'citoen' of the republic . . . that means you are not in a republic in England. [laughter]

KM: I know, we have a queen and all that.

PS: My work is sometimes that of an explorer. Or I am a politic agent – a terrorist if you want.

KM: But you designed the Mitterrand interior.

PS: But it's left, you know, it's left. But I am not a terrorist because terrorism is negative, I am just subversive.

KM: Right, so not an anarchist! In the Royalton building you have designed an interior with intelligent features such as an automatically flushing WC. Will you continue to explore intelligent technology in your buildings in the future? More computers . . . ?

PS: More computers – I don't know. No, I am not in the trend of that, I am a little suspicious. I don't want to say that the computer isn't good. The computer is the future on the desk of humanity, it is incredibly powerful. I love computer images, how else can we have shapes like Nani Nani? Nobody can say the computer is bad, but I do not believe in the 'computer house', if I can say that. I don't believe in it because we need life; yes, we need life. But if the computer can drive the heater well, why not?

KM: But you have a plan to insert a computer into the skin under the forearm. Surely that shows that you are keen to use more technology in a less utilitarian way than you just described?

PS: No, that I completely believe in. I have been working on it for more than fifteen years. I think it will be realised next year. We have all the elements to do it: we know how to put the metal under the skin, we know how to make the energy, we know how to make the skin transparent. No, that is very important because it is the theory of inspiration one more time. We need life, but we won't be God. That means we will be powerful, intelligent, communicant. We need all that because today it is stupid not to speak immediately with intelligence in other parts of the world. But when you are in front of a big computer you are not in the best position for that, which is why I want people to have all the power a computer can give, but to be in the best position to think or to dream. So that if somebody's best way to live, best biorhythm, is to be naked on the beach, why not? Completely for this reason I believe in

the internal computer. I am not alone, it was my dream 15 years ago, now 20 years ago. A Japanese company has discovered a direct connection with the brain through a prototype where you can drive the computer with the brain directly. A lot of people have steel in their legs, or a plastic heart, it is easy to solve that.

KM: But do you think that we are getting away from nature doing that – what sort of an effect will it have on us as humans?

PS: No, I think today that we are against nature. Today we are still in the century of the material, that means we still are in the 19th century. With the dust, the mechanic, the smell of the warm oil, the sweat. That is bad for man and it is bad for nature. If we continue to have less materials to have more power we shall come back and we can keep real nature. A real one.

KM: Some of your buildings look organic or even anthropomorphic – the Nani Nani building which looks like an animal, for instance, makes you feel close to nature in that the shapes are familiar but the technology used to achieve the shape does not appear natural. How do you combine the two?

PS: I must say, I live completely in nature. I live in the middle of a big forest, or on a houseboat in a field of mud in my oyster company in the middle of 200 million oysters, fish and crabs. I try to connect directly with the idea of God which is the only human dream, and the idea of nature without the material. And that is easy, it is the only way.

KM: Do you agree with what Franco Bertoni wrote about your Nani Nani building?

PS: I read nothing about architecture.

KM: Bertoni said that he would be scared to be alone in the Nani Nani building at night.

PS: I hope so. If it is true it is perfect because it is done for that reason: imagine you walk in a Tokyo street at night and suddenly you see a huge green monster, it is definitely more interesting than seeing a regular building. It is 30 seconds of something else, of a new adventure.

KM: Some of your buildings do not seem to have many windows. Do you think it is important to use energy from the sun and wind in buildings?

PS: I believe only in the window and the sun. If you think specifically about the building where you don't see the windows, called Le Baron Vert, Osaka, it is because it is designed with trickery.

If you are inside the building it is completely glass and you are wholly in the sun.

KM: And the Ashai building?

PS: The Ashai building is a commercial building. This means that there are windows everywhere; there is a window of one-metre diameter every five metres – a lot of windows. But a little less than the other because sometimes we need darkness inside, for theatre and things like that. It is technical. I believe only in animals. We are animals, and animals need sun definitely. I am working in my new house, the first day, and it is completely in glass.

KM: The one in the Maison Suisse?

PS: No this is the one in Paris, the Rue Starck. The one you are thinking of is in the forest.

KM: Do you think that a lot of people will buy the one through the catologue?

PS: Oh yes, they do.

KM: It seems to me to be very expensive.

PS: No, it is not expensive in France. For Americans and English it is expensive because construction is not the same in England and the USA. In the USA the house costs strictly nothing but it is bullshit made of paper. France has a regular price for all the popular houses. My target was very simple. I was trying to provide alternative solutions for people because today all the big companies produce and sell the same bullshit. My target was to make trouble for these big companies. That is all, not more. That is when I decided on this war, especially in France. I went to the showrooms of these people, took the price, the measurement, the programme, and I asked every company what people tend to buy. I then made exactly the same thing, with the same surface, the same price, but with love and quality, that's all.

KM: Your father designed aircraft and apparently you are very interested in planes. Do you know the Stealth bomber, what do you think of it? Do you think that it shows how we will travel in the future?

PS: The invisible plane, oh no, because it is a plane of observation. But you know that the Stealth plane is not good as a tactical weapon. No, it is not true. The main reason for the Stealth's existence is that the president of the USA can decide two hours later to press on the bomber [the bomb]. That is very important for our world. That is why it is a positive product. And for me it is the most beautiful product that people have invented at the leading edge of technology. The Stealth has an incredible quality. Firstly, it is invisible, strong. Secondly, it can convey a different image of itself. That is its talent. Thirdly, it can send an image it designs at 4000km from where it is – pure poetry. I can't imagine the human intelligence doing that.

KM: How would you design a plane?

PS: We are already working on one. Again it is political. We want to kill the price of planes. And today the two-engine plane – it is good to have two engines because of safety – costs a little less than one million dollars. And we shall produce one which will cost a little less than 100,000 dollars. As for the big countries which have no money – such as South America, Africa, China – because all these countries needs spare ambulances, I don't know what. And today we can produce a 'jeep of the air' very cheaply, which is easy to maintain. I fly myself on the prototype of that. After tomorrow, I will try the new product.

KM: Good luck.

PS: I crashed in May. It was terrible.

KM: In a plane?

PS: Oh yes, I crashed terribly, but it was funny.

KM: But you weren't hurt?

PS: No, nothing. It was very interesting. It was an extreme excercise. We flew very low and suddenly we fell out of the sky like a stone.

KM: How terrifying!

PS: No, no, no, it was funny.

CHRISTO AND JEANNE-CLAUDE

WRAPPING THE REICHSTAG

Wrapping is an old idea which we no longer do. Neither the *Valley Curtain* nor *The Umbrellas* can be described as such. A project that took a long time, like the Pont Neuf, was the last Wrapping idea. It originated in 1975 but was carried out in 1985 – it took us 10 years to convince the French people. The Reichstag, like all the projects, will only be wrapped for two weeks. The installation will be very fast – four to five days. We pay for all the expenses of our projects, without sponsors.

We use man-made fabric; organic fibre is not strong enough to resist abrasion and wind forces. The colour silver was chosen so that even on a grey day when the building is just a silhouette in the landscape its volume and presence will be increased; the reflection between shade and light creates such strong contrasts. Also, we want to have very right-angled, almost medieval gothic pleats and folds. Like the Pont Neuf, the Reichstag fabric highlights the principal proportion of the building: the volume of the towers or proportion of the facade. All details disappear, hidden behind the fabric.

The projects are bigger than our imaginations. Everything which belonged to the Reichstag until 1989 will continue to do so, but with the end of the Cold War, the fall of the wall, a new dimension exists. What is exciting about these projects – the Reichstag or *The Umbrellas* – is their tremendous power. We cannot argue that we know fully how the Japanese see the blue Umbrellas in Japan for we are not Japanese ourselves. In the same way, it is difficult for us to say how the Germans will view the *Wrapped Reichstag*. However, it is lucky the project was not done before '89 because the Reichstag would have been like a footnote during the Cold War, and its wrapping associated with showing the Communist world how the West do things. The building was like a mausoleum: a structure that couldn't be used, with no future. What's exciting is that it now has a future.

During the wrapped project, the fabric moves dynamically. Thus the nomadic quality of this project will be translated, which is important. The fabrication of the wrapping material – the sewing of the fabric – will be designed with very intricate patterns in 70 sections by our chief engineering company. When the wrapping begins, all the material will be on top of the building. Around 125-150 construction workers will be involved, people who work building bridges and high-rise buildings, and an additional 200 rock climbers unfolding the rolls of fabric simultaneously from the building's four facades. They follow the fabric on their ropes to lace sections together and secure the artistic ropes. At ground level will be the non-skilled workers, art students, architectural students – 450 of them – controlling the movement of the fabric. Three to five days later everything is ready.

Our projects have two distinct periods: software and hardware. The former is when the project exists only through drawings. There are many facets of this period, not only with the Reichstag. When we started with the blue Umbrellas in Japan – 1, 340 of them – we had to lease the land which was 12 miles long and two-and-a-half miles wide from 459 Japanese rice farmers. The youngest was 65 and the oldest 89. We spent two-and-a-half years talking to the farmers about using their rice fields. Each occasion requires such incredible negotiation. We learn so much with every project, it is like university for us and the many friends involved.

Now we are experiencing the Reichstag which is owned by 80 million Germans – we cannot in a lifetime talk to this number of people! Fortunately they are represented by 662 deputies in Parliament. To obtain the majority required explaining the project, three points in particular. Firstly, that we had been doing works of art all our lives, not agricultural fences or industrial constructions even though they look strange; they are created in rural and city places but are works of art. The work of art benefits from its space which is not in a museum or gallery but is space with tremendous order, jurisdictions and ownership; also the *Valley Curtain* or the *Running Fence* are dealing with proportion, colours and volume. Our optimism is reflected in the dynamic and positive nature of the projects. The *Valley Curtain* created a magnetic situation, as did *The Umbrellas* and *The Pont Neuf Wrapped* – we would like to do the same thing with the Reichstag. This will be different but will deal with proportion and colours. Wrapped objects are like living objects as they move with the wind and are very sensual and inviting. They create some urgency to be seen because tomorrow they will be gone.

Historically the Reichstag features in political history books but when wrapped it will be in history of art books. We explained this to the Bundestag, along with the long tradition of artists fascinated by architecture: Piranesi, Raphael and Claude Monet who painted Chartres Cathedral. Unlike Monet we take the real building and effect a temporary change. A member of the Christian Socialist Union, Mr Hans Klein, said that supporting the project would be political suicide for him, while Mr Freimut Duve claimed it was very important and uplifting; able to provoke a smile and an attitude lacking in the German people. Some members of the Bundestag are very knowledgeable. Mr Peter Conradi, by profession an architect, is very excited with a much deeper involvement.

I like to draw not just to finance the project but to reveal how it is crystallised visually and has changed through the years, as I learn more about the building, the light and the movement. My engineers design the patterns by computer but all drawing is done by hand, my own right hand.

Like the Pont Neuf and the people who were walking over the bridge the building will be fully functional. The project is always filmed. The Reichstag has been filmed by Maysles since the mid '70s. We have historical meetings with Mr Willy Brandt and others no longer alive, they are all part of the incredible archives.

We don't know yet to whom we dedicate the project, but acknowledge greatly the German deputies for debating for the first time in the history of parliamentarianism a work of art – not only for one-and-a-half hours but entirely live, transmitted to the entire common market, 200 million people. A member for the Green Environmentalist Party said how refreshing and stimulating it was to talk about aesthetics and art, rather than Somalia, Bosnia or unemployment

I remember one of Mr Willy Brandt's comments early on in the Reichstag project describing how it was closer to the German soul than other projects had been to host nations and would engage an entire nation. We are borrowing not only the Reichstag but a very rich space. You walk outside and in the street somebody designed the side-walk, the road, even the airspace. The space is highly controlled, designed by the regulations of politicians and urban planners; it is so resourceful, unpredictable, complex, so real. Nothing is make-believe: real fear, real forces – so different from safe playing 'in the art media'. Similarly with the Pont Neuf in late September 1985, two months after a huge terrorist attack in Paris when 17 people were killed in a synagogue, there was a tremendous political risk that the Pont Neuf would be used by terrorists. It was passed through by Mr Gorbachev on his first visit to the West.

The first objects I wrapped in '58 were small, humble objects. The first outdoor public work was *Dockside Packages* at Cologne harbour in 1961. The Reichstag project concerns a public building, thus involving the full democratic process. We wrote twice to Chancellor Kohl. He never answered our letters but said to the Press in early January 1994 that the ambivalent and complex history of the Reichstag denied it as a subject for art and that it would create imbalance and would be very unhealthy for the nation. We wrote a response, published in many German newspapers, stating that anything in the world can be a subject of art from humble flowers to the image of Jesus Christ and God. I can't believe that any German in his right mind thinks the Reichstag is more important than God.

The Central Park project, *The Gates*, was turned down in 1981 with three major objections. Park commissioner, Mr Gordon Davis, was a lawyer. Typical to the profession, the first objection was very legal: that the project would create a precedent and a line of artists requesting permission to use Central Park. Secondly, it would attract too many people. However, even though we used 26 miles of walkways – in the entire park from North, South, East and West – there would not have been a concentration of millions of people in one place. Thirdly, he was flabbergasted that eight million could be spent on a temporary work of art, even if paid for by us.

These projects stem from our wish to enlarge and question the notion of art. Several projects have elements of painting: the pink fabric floating on the surface of the water of the *Surrounded Islands* is like abstract canvas, flat with no volume. Some have very strong notions based on sculpture, such as the Pont Neuf bridge in Paris, a classical sculpture done in fabric rather than marble or stone. The Pont Neuf was also architecture: the installation of thousands of umbrellas akin to urbanism, each one the size of a two-storey house, 640 square feet; like building miles and miles of villages. Architecture, urbanism, painting, sculpture, all play together.

The character of the project challenges the immortality of art, building things in steel and gold to be remembered forever. It is probably more courageous to go away than to stay. Nobody can sell tickets for what we create. We don't own these projects. They cannot stay because freedom is the enemy of possession and possession is the equal of permanence.

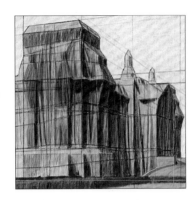

The unfurling of the fabric and installation of the ropes for the 'Wrapped Reichstag: Berlin 1971-95' will start on June 17th 1995, weather permitting. Completion of the work of art will be around or before June 23rd, 1995. It will be wrapped for 14 days.

Drawing in two parts (38 x 244cm and 106.6 x 244cm); collage in two parts (77.5 x 66.7cm and 77.5 x 30.5cm), Wrapped Reichstag, project for Berlin © Christo, 1992. Photographs by Wolfgang Volz

reviews *books*

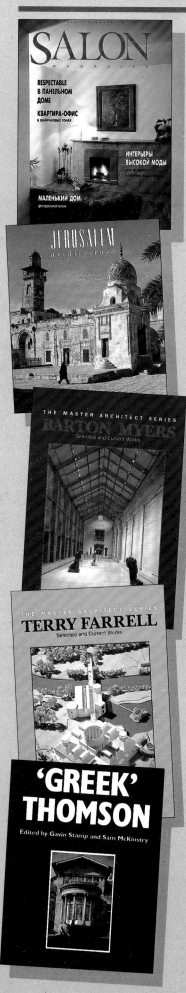

SALON New Russian architecture/interior decoration magazine, Galina V Main Associates, Julius-Reiber-Strasse 16, D-64293 Darmstadt, Germany
Salon is the first Russian periodical to cover trends in residential and commercial architecture and interior decoration in that country. A publication of this nature would have been unthinkable as recently as a few years ago, in view of the lack of anything beyond drab, state-owned dwellings at that time, and its publishers and editors are to be commended for having brokent the ice and taken the risk of introducing a well written, exquisitely photographed, and lavishly produced magazine covering the rapid developments that have transpired since the fall of communism. Subsequent economic reforms have resulted in new found demands for dwellings that meet the standards prevalent elsewhere around Europe; Russian architects and interior decorators have clearly wasted no time in response.

The premier issue contains Russian-language articles covering the interiors of a number of private dwellings and commercial buildings that have been redcorated employing exclusively domestically available materials. One article features a private home near Moscow that has been rebuilt in postmodern style while maintaining national traditions. Others feature the interior of 'Dom Modelii', a Moscow hotel on Kachalov Street, whose interior decorators have made generous use of motifs from Russian classicism, and Moscow's 'English Club' an impressive project displaying ample historical allusions. Coverage is restricted to recently completed, professionally planned and supervised, restoration and renovation projects displaying high degrees of creativity and originality. Those featured are indeed impressive, and should dispel any doubts regarding the talents and abilities of Russian architects and interior decorators. This bodes well for the rebirth of Russian architecture and interior decoration its publishers are clearly counting on.

JERUSALEM ARCHITECTURE by David Kroyanker, Tauris Parke Books, 200pp, colour ills, HB £38
The author describes the history of Jerusalem through its architecture, revealing how the urban fabric of this sacred city, venerated by Jews, Christians and Muslims alike is characterised by buildings of 3,000 years ago next to those of the present day. New Jerusalem is outside the city walls which were built in the 16th century by Suleiman the magnificent. It involves the huge convents, hospitals, schools and churches erected by European Christians, the first ethnic Jewish neighborhoods, the lavish villas of affluent Arabs, the garden suburbs developed during the 1930s and the enlightened as well as elegant building and planning carried out under the British mandate. Modern Jerusalem emerges in the large campuses of the Hebrew University, the Government Precinct, and the unremitting attempt to achieve both quality and economy in the domain of mass housing. under discussion is the ongoing search for a style of modern architecture unique to Jerusalem and worthy of its extraordinary antecedents.

BARTON MYERS Selected and Current Works, introduced by John R Dale, Master Architect Series, Images Publishing, 255pp, colour ills, HB £40
Myers' increasing focus on the design of performing arts facilities is an appropriate outcome of 25 years of practice. Two of his major projects: the Cerritos Centre for the performing Arts and the New Jersey Performing Arts Centre are examined here. While Myers' practice continues to address a diverse range of urban design, planning and building projects, it is in the venue of the theatre, whether as a room for concerts or a stage for drama, that so many of the themes and preoccupations of his work naturally come into play with each other. He considers the theatre to be one of civilisation's greatest institutions, its performance space the best of all urban rooms, because of its ability to unite a diverse citizenry with the arts at a single point in time and space.

TERRY FARRELL Selected and Current Works, introduced by Clare Melhuish, Master Architect Series, Images Publishing, 255pp, colour ills, HB £40
Terry Farrell asserts that his main aim is to try and design from the inside out as well as the outside in. He seeks to base his work on construction, use and function as well as the context: the influence of the people and the place. In the past, the MI6 Vauxhall Cross building has been questioned concerning this philosophy. Farrell claims that 'The architect's task is to develop form which follows function but also from flowing context. It is not a question of choosing between the two but of doing both, which requires more skill and creativity. It produces a more hybrid language and a cross-cultural type of building, but to try to produce an architecture which follows only one rule, whether constructional or functional, is simply escapist.' The importance he places on context, as opposed to function is thought provoking in an age where post-functional design is seldom a topic that reaches discussion.

'GREEK' THOMPSON edited by Gavin Stamp and Sam McKinstry, Edinburgh University Press, 300pp, b/w ills, HB £35
This book, introduced by John Summerson, is a useful and interesting examination of the work of Alexander 'Greek' Thomson, a great intellectual and key exponent of the Greek Revival, who, to some extent has been eclipsed by fellow Glaswegian designer Charles Rennie Mackintosh. This was not always so, as revealed in the collection of essays reviewing the background, theory and ideals, urbanism, interiors and the international dimension. Thomson, like Mackintosh, was also celebrated for other media such as cast iron, wallpaper, textiles and furniture as well as architecture; a chapter within, devoted to his furniture, indicates that it was always designed for a specific location to correspond with other elements of the interior. That the architect should be 'equally conversant' with the building and furnishing of a

house was advocated by J C Loudon (1839). At a time when anything 'Grecian' was the rage, it emerges that Thomson was provided with a certain amount of freedom to produce innovative designs for his fashion-conscious clients. It is interesting that few references in his surviving writings on architecture are made to specific foreign architects or buildings; apparently he found more to excite him in modern painting and, like Schinkel, paintings of imaginative architectural panoramas were of great inspiration to him. According to Thomson the Acropolis of Athens was, 'one of the most glorious sights which the human eye has ever been permitted to behold, and the like of which it will never again see in this world'.

HOUSING WOMEN edited by Rose Gilroy and Roberta Woods, Routledge, 278pp, HB £37.50/PB £12.99

What impact has housing policy had on women? Introduced in this book are key issues concerning housing for women in an industry which is male-dominated. Of interest to students and researchers in social policy, housing, architecture and women's studies, this publication aims to build upon those issues addressed by past literature and to draw together the diverse strands of women's housing experiences. The first four chapters consider the general themes of access, participation and the meaning of 'home'. Chapters five to eight address the housing concerns of specific groups of women. Chapters nine and ten look at education, training and employment issues. Chapters eleven and twelve present innovative housing designs, revealing alternatives in the USA to the single family house and neighbourhood: 'cohousing' and residential developments which combine common and private spaces, space to live, work and possibly rent out, and private rooms with adjacent collective day care; responding to the need for housing with integrated support services of a transitional rather than permanent nature. Imaginative ideas examined here, which are engendered by full involvement in the process, include self-building and 'green design'.

INTERNATIONAL TERRITORY The United Nations 1945-95 by Adam Bartos and Christopher Hitchens, Verso, 104pp, colour ills, HB £19.95

'If the Secretariat building will have anything to say as a symbol it will be, I fear, that the managerial revolution has taken place and that bureaucracy rules the world.' (Lewis Mumford, 1947.) The UN building has been the focus of international inspiration for half a century. Its podium has seen petitioners for peace, for independence, for justice; its murals and statuary express the loftiest ideals. The most optimistic elements of modernism in design were enshrined and symbolised here in function, but it was also an occasion of dispute between the Rockefellers and Le Corbusier; thus indirectly, between two conceptions of world order. A series of evocative colour photos documents exterior and interior views, capturing an interesting range of details throughout the building, while attesting to the wear and tear of an idealism thwarted by decades of diplomatic compromise. Themes of Utopia and the limits of governmental good intentions are explored in the preceding text.

WRIGHT IN HOLLYWOOD Visions of a New Architecture by Robert L Sweeney, MIT Press, 300pp, colour ills, HB £45.95

Amidst the proliferation of books on the work of Wright, another new focus arises, this time probing an aspect of his design which has never entered the mainstream of architectural discourse: the so-called textile block system. Wright had been forming this gradually in his mind since he returned from Japan after work on the Imperial Hotel, and between 1922 and 1932 he pursued this avidly. After initial experiments in southern California Wright was soon able to demonstrate that the system was capable of a more universal application. In his hands it became far more than a method of building with concrete block. Henry-Russell Hitchcock referred to Wright's work with this system in the 1920s, surmising that, 'since 1923, the technical aspect of his work in California has been of the utmost importance'. Though he praised within two years the potential of the method for Wright's use of ornament, Hitchcock continued: 'Although this formula [casting designs into blocks themselves] is far from the "pure ornamentation" suitable for the Age of the Machine, it is more discrete and of a healthier originality than badly understood cubism or the exoticism of the immediately preceding decorative works'.

ONTOLOGY OF CONSTRUCTION On Nihilism of Technology in Theories of Modern Architecture by Gevork Hartoonian, Cambridge University Press, 120pp, b/w ills, HB £27.95

This book outlines that theories of construction in modern architecture are explored with particular focus on the relationship between nihilism of technology and architecture. Providing a historical context for the concept of 'making', the essays collected in this volume articulate the implications of technology in works by such architects as Le Corbusier, Wright, Loos, and Mies van der Rohe. An interpretation is provided of Gottfried Semper's discourse on the tectonic and the relationship between architecture and other crafts. Emphasised as a critical theme for contemporary artchitectural theory and practice is 'fabrication' is. The foreword is by Kenneth Frampton.

ISLAMIC ARCHITECTURE by Rovert Hillebrand, Edinburgh University Press, 640pp, b/w and colour ills, HB £49.50

This extensive volume surveys in a novel way the major building types of the Islamic World spanning from *c*700 to *c*1700: religious architecture (the mosque, the minaret, the madrasa), the mausoleum 'between Heaven and Earth', and in the secular field the caravansarai and the palace. The interplay of form and function is taken as the underlying theme of the analysis. The authoritative text is accompanied by analytical and comparative drawings, ground plans and photographs. Referential and supplementary information is also provided by glossaries of Islamic terms and key indexes by individual monument, name and subject.

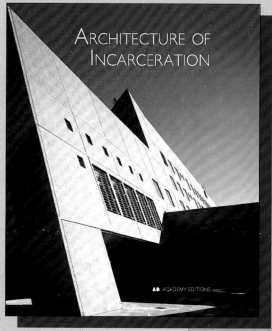

ARCHITECTURE OF INCARCERATION

This unique volume looks at developments in the design of prisons, an area of architecture which remains relatively underexposed in the light of changes that have taken place this century, and which is currently experiencing a high level of constructional activity in response to overcrowding and rising crime rates. The selection of essays provides an insight into the traditional aspects of prison architecture – from its development in the late eighteenth century and rigid nineteenth-century diffusions, wherein communication between prisons was severed – through to the contemporary condition. Featuring drawings and strong colour images of recently executed and projected designs, low, medium and maximum security institutions are viewed within the framework of their architectural structure.

The body of projects illustrates both built and unbuilt schemes which exist in a variety of countries, working explicitly towards the creation of a particular environment. Typological studies also indicate some of the problems involved in designing correctional facilities. *Architecture of Incarceration* is a thought-provoking publication, providing stimulating source material in accessible form of a subject that has engendered a variety of design interpretations, each one responding to a brief that is universally challenging. Foreword by Judge Tumim, HM Chief Inspector of Prisons

Hardback 1 85490 358 6
305 x 252 mm, 128 pages
Over 290 illustrations, mainly in colour
Publication: November 1994

First published in 1973, this definitive documentation, with excerpts from the Family Recollections by Hermine Wittgenstein, focuses on the Wittgenstein House in Vienna. Declared a national monument in 1972 by the Vienna Landmark Commission it was faithfully restored in 1973. Ludwig Wittgenstein designed the house for his sister in 1927-28. Although he had no professional architectural qualifications the interior of this building is quite unique. Every detail has been rethought and appears to be uninfluenced by any building convention or style. The cubic forms of the building's exterior reveal the influence of his friend the Viennese architect Adolf Loos. This accurate record contains drawings and

photographs of the original work, including details of the metal door frames, lifts and internal fittings so important to Wittgenstein's concept. Illustrated throughout, it is the key documentation of the work of Ludwig Wittgenstein, the world famous Austrian philosopher who taught at Cambridge and is celebrated for his interest and writings on architecture. The book was originally produced in collaboration with the Wittgenstein family, relatives and friends.

Historical Buildings Monograph
Paperback 1 85490 414 0
252 x 190 mm, 128 pages,
Extensively illustrated
Publication: June 1995

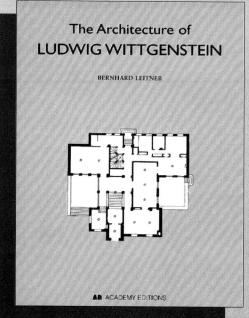

The Architecture of
LUDWIG WITTGENSTEIN

BERNHARD LEITNER

The powerful imagery of the revolutionary Russian artists and architects of the 1920's still remains highly popular today; however, many of the underlying theories of these artists and designers are only available in Russian language form and remain widely unexplored. Through a series of collected essays, many appearing in English for the first time, the world renowned expert on Russian Avant-Garde architecture, Catherine Cooke, focuses on these underlying concepts and theories and explores the new approaches to art and architecture in the modern society, the aesthetic and social impact of mass production, new technologies, new communications. This highly illustrated volume contains clear accounts of the theories of such artists as Kandinsky, Malevich, Tatlin and Rodchenko and of key modernist architects such as Melnikhov, the Constructivists and the Rationalists.

Paperback 1 85490 390 X
305 x 252 mm 208 pages
Illustrated throughout
Publication: April 1995

There are many intense debates within schools of architecture throughout the world. One of the most controversial topics for discussion is the process of educating an architect. The text, generated at an international symposium of architectural educators held at the University of Portsmouth School of Architecture in the UK, explores this and other topical issues. Divided into two parts, this book initially charts the history of architectural education and examines the diverse variety of approaches and ideologies towards the teaching of architecture today. It then presents a range of educational methodologies from Post-Structural theory to craft-based Ruskinian practice. Many of the most influential contemporary architects are both educators and practising architects: contributors include Bernard Tschumi, Lebbeus Woods, Daniel Libeskind and Rob Krier, who present their own models for the future of education.

As the ideals and priorites taught in schools shape our future architects, this book provides an insight in to the state of architecture tomorrow. Aimed at both students and teachers, it will also be of interest to anyone involved in the progress of architecture.

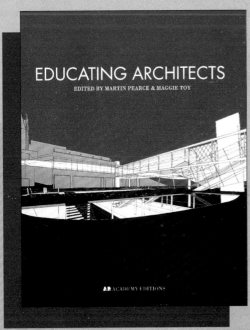

Paperback 1 85490 391 8
279 x 217 mm 144 pages
Extensively illustrated
Publication: April 1995

Further information can be obtained from Academy Group Ltd. Tel: 071 402 2141 Fax: 071 723 9540

LINA BO BARDI

Elisabetta Andreoli

Lina started her career in Italy, in the 1940s, working with the Italian architect and designer Gio Ponti. In 1946 she moved to Brazil with her husband, the art historian Pietro Maria Bardi. Although never fully accepted by the Academia, because of both her political positions and strong provocative personality, Lina designed some of the most interesting works of Modern architecture to be found in Brazil.

The Museum of Art of Sao Paulo (MASP) built in 1958 was a most daring work in terms of both engineering and imagination. The innovative formal and structural solutions adopted turned it into a major point of reference for Sao Paulo citizens for cultural, political and leisure activities.

The SESC, Pompeia (1977) involved the recuperation of an abandoned factory located in a fairly industrial part of the town. With minimal alterations of the original structure of the factory, built in iron and bricks, Lina provided the building with a number of facilities including workshops, two restaurants, a theatre and open areas for recreation, pastime, games, reading and exhibitions. On the small area available outside the factory Lina added two massive buildings hosting a large number of sports facilities. The austere and almost brutal aspect of their concrete structure – that fits well with the industrial surroundings – is strongly mitigated by the irregular shapes of the huge windows. From inside the building, these 'holes' that look like Matisse's cut-outs provide unexpected poetical views of this most chaotic industrial town. SESC, Pompeia is today an extremely popular and pleasant leisure centre for people of all ages.

Other than in Sao Paulo, Lina also worked in the northern town of Salvador, capital of Bahia. Her projects illustrate a great degree of perceptiveness in dealing with the predominantly black local culture and she won the affection and admiration of many Bahianos.

The variety of formal solutions adopted in her projects indicates that Lina was able to combine the lessons of Modernism, which she had fully assimilated during her time in Italy – with a deep understanding of some of the most salient aspects of Brazilian nature and culture. She always insisted that many of her ideas and solutions had actually derived from the world of Brazilian popular culture.

Her approach led her to work in different fields – organising exhibitions and workshops, designing theatre stages and costumes as well as furniture for both private and public spaces. This was often done in conjunction with artists, singers, theatre and film directors, who were fighting their way against both a conservative and a folkloric approach to art and culture. Her knowledge and appreciation of popular cullture did not focus on 'frozen' forms and materials but on the creative processes and solutions invented by the people in the effort to improve their material and spiritual well-being.

What is interesting about the exhibition is that some of the themes discussed currently in the fields of art and architecture – such as the critique of Modernism, the recognition of different voices and the questioning of eurocentric notions – seem to have been addressed by Lina's architectural approach. Her work thus provides food for thought concerning relevant issues today. The exhibition is an opportunity to appreciate that there is more to Brazilian architecture than the work of Oscar Niemeyer. In fact, in many respects the works of these two architects are almost antagonistic. Niemeyer's monumental architecture seems to symbolise a distant power whereas Lina's is the architecture of social interaction and conviviality.

The Olympo of modern architecture is inhabited almost exclusively by male gods. Although anti-feminism was part of Lina's controversial attitudes, we should nonetheless welcome the sudden appearance of a great female modern architect.

The travelling exhibition, 'The Life and Works of Lina Bo Bardi 1914-92', is at Espace de la SIP, Geneva, March 1995

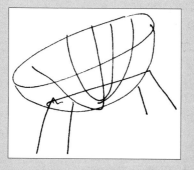

ABOVE: SESC, Pompeia logotype 'a seal of popular communication, and not an abstract monogram (so over-used today, see the acronyms for construction companies, government entities etc). It represents the water tower/chimney of the Pompeia Center. Instead of smoke, the tower-chimney sends out flowers. The flower-chimney sending out flowers shall be the emblem of the center: reproduced on stickers of various sizes to be applied on cars, on printed forms, on plates and glasses and embroidered onto workers' uniforms. It is important that the colours be red and black, with a great visual impact . . . the word 'factory' should appear in the logo, as it is the dialectic significance of work-leisure.' BELOW: Bardi's Bowl, chair design, 1951

THE POWER OF ARCHITECTURE

JOHANN OTTO VON SPRECKELSEN, L'ARCHE DE LA DÉFENSE, PARIS

Architectural Design

THE POWER OF ARCHITECTURE

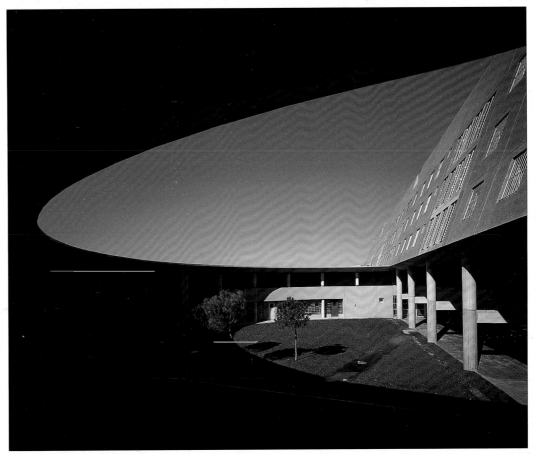

RÉMY BUTLER, MAISON D'ARRET, BREST; *OPPOSITE*: PETER KULKA, THE SAXON PARLIAMENT, DRESDEN

ACADEMY EDITIONS • LONDON

Acknowledgements

All material is courtesy of the authors and architects unless otherwise stated.

'What Do Buildings Have To Do With Power' is adapted from chapter one of *Buildings and Power: Freedom and Control in the Origin of Modern Building Types*, Thomas A Markus, Routledge, London, 1993, reproduced with the publishers' permission. Illustration *p10*, source: item AE II 3076, French National Archives, Paris. Illustration *p15*, source: redrawn from Hillier and Hanson, 1984. Illustration *p16*, source: Soane Collection 32 (33) by courtesy of the RCAHMS and the Trustees of Sir John Soane's Museum. Illustration p17 above, source: author's drawing based on original by Salaman Othman, redrawn for *Environment and Planning B: Planning and Design*, 1987. Illustration *p17* below, source: Stark, 1807, Glasgow District Council, Mitchell Library. Illustration *p18*, source: Stiftsbibliotek St Gallen. 'Philip Johnson' is adapted from the chapters 'Peter', 'Decon' and 'Burgee: Discarded by the Discarded' from *Philip Johnson, Life and Work*, Franz Schuzle, Alfred A Knopff Inc, New York, 1994, reproduced with the publishers' permission. Kim Dovey, 'Place/Power' is a revised version of 'Place, Power and Ideology' first published in *Transition*, 35, RMIT, Melbourne, 1991, reproduced with the publishers' permission. 'Parliament House' is a revised version of 'Canberra Interrotta – Giurgola's Design For Parliament House', *The Age Monthly Review*, Melbourne. Illustrations *p56* source: The Museum of Finnish Architecture, Helsinki, Finland. The text for the Dutch Parliament is written by Jan Rutten, first published in *New Second Chamber of Parliament Building*, Amsterdam. 'Hôtel du Département des Bouches du Rhone' is adapted from *Le Grand Bleu*, Michael Spens, Academy Editions, London, 1994. This is also available in a several languages edition by Ernst and Sohn, Berlin and in French language edition, distributed in France by Interart, Paris. We are grateful to Sherry Bates and Katerina Ruedi for their help in selecting relevant students from Kingston University.

Front Cover: Alsop and Störmer, Hôtel du Département des Bouches du Rhone, Marseilles
Inside Covers: Daniel Libeskind, 'Powerp', *Architecture I*

Photographic Credits
All material is courtesy of the authors and architects unless otherwise stated.
Paul Raftery *Front Cover*, Charles Jencks *pp1, 29*, Jörg Schöner *p2*, Richard Einzig *pp6, 26*, Luc Boegly/Archipress *p27*, Mario Bettella *p28*, Ian Davidson *p39 below*, Sarah Heath *p40 above*, Jeff Goldberg *pp46-49*, Jussi Tiainen *pp50-51 except centre left*, Sarlotta Narjus *p50 centre left*, J Gollings *pp52, 54 right*, R Giurgola *p54*, Fridtof Versnel *pp58-59*, Richard Davies *pp62-63*, Tom Bonner *pp78-79*, Deidi von Schaewen *pp3, 80-83*, Tomas Riehle *p84*, Henryk Urbanietz *p85*, HG Esch *p86*, Lukas Roth *p87*

EDITOR: Maggie Toy
EDITORIAL TEAM: Iona Spens, Katherine MacInnes, Stephen Watt
ART EDITOR: Andrea Bettella CHIEF DESIGNER: Mario Bettella DESIGNER: Toby Norman

CONSULTANTS: Catherine Cooke, Terry Farrell, Kenneth Frampton, Charles Jencks, Heinrich Klotz, Leon Krier, Robert Maxwell, Demetri Porphyrios, Kenneth Powell, Colin Rowe, Derek Walker

First published in Great Britain in 1995 by *Architectural Design* an imprint of
ACADEMY GROUP LTD, 42 LEINSTER GARDENS, LONDON W2 3AN
Member of the VCH Publishing Group
ISBN: 1 85490 248 2 (UK)

Architectural Design Profile 114 is published as part of *Architectural Design* Vol 65 3-4/1995
Architectural Design Magazine is published six times a year and is available by subscription

Distributed to the trade in the United States of America by
ST MARTIN'S PRESS, 175 FIFTH AVENUE, NEW YORK, NY 10010

Printed and bound in Italy

Contents

ARCHITECTURAL DESIGN PROFILE No 114

THE POWER OF ARCHITECTURE

EDITORIAL

Maggie Toy

A perpetual relationship exists between architecture and power, which is open to a variety of interpretations. Architects are renowned for expressing their power over the building site and government leaders have been known to use their architects to exert power over the population. The meaning communicated by an architectural language can change dramatically. For example, the Classical dialect adopted by Adolf Hitler and Albert Speer in the 1930s, had been used since the time of the ancient Greeks to indicate the power of democracy. The events of the Second World War caused these buildings to become associated with the beliefs of a distinctly unpleasant fascist regime; any client patronising a particular style needs to be aware of its connotations. Such is the strength of architectural interpretation.

It is interesting, therefore, to examine the way architecture conveys political ideals world-wide and to understand what governments are saying to their electorate. Australia makes a clear statement with its recently completed Parliament House, the oversized flag is flown high over the great sweeping curve of the side walls which embrace all who enter here. Germany's message is more ambiguous. It concerns the alterations to the Reichstag – the hard-fought competition providing a solution that reconciles history with an unknown future. The series of *Grand Projets* in France projects a progressive, forward-thinking political image to the world that is extremely influential, even through successive governments, and has become identified as the people's choice. Erica Winterbourne discusses the benefits made possible through appropriately applied architectural patronage and the power of patrons to control the future of the built environment. A prequisite for a futuristic utopia is optimism about the future, and the attitude of the French shines through its cultural, architectural symbols.

Appropriate architectural language can therefore communicate whatever type of government to its people. However, the language is equally exploited by the corporate prerogative as it is by government bodies. Architecture helps establish a cultural identity and therefore announces to the world the desired company image. This notion is often linked with another expression of power which accompanies the commissioning of

architecture. The corporate and governmental status controls both the architect and the building.

In the manipulation of the built environment, Philip Johnson has continued to demonstrate architectural power for the majority of this century. He therefore commands serious consideration in this issue, challenging Foucault's observation that: 'power is usually more dispersed than we think'; or perhaps what has worked for Johnson is 'the trick', which in Foucault's words is: 'to let people assume it is concentrated'.

A considerable number of architects desire the power of an ideology. The power held by an architect whose ideas are discussed internationally and whose designs are imitated frequently is of a very seductive nature. Few buildings attain a world-wide reputation and even fewer are canonised into architectural history. Many architects crave to be recognised as possessing the skill and talent necessary to create one of the few buildings which not only satisfies the client on a practical level but also has the ability to touch a deeper intellectual interpretation and become a model for others to emulate. The architects perceived as such hold an incredible power over architects and clients.

There is also a specific and obvious allocation of power within buildings. Thomas Markus demonstrates through the specific examples of monasteries, law courts and concert halls the clarity of power expressed through functions within buildings. Power is relative to specific cultural and historic conditions. The strongest form of control is negative power, which is fear. In selected building forms this is used consciously to suit the purpose of the building.

Control within the building has varying degrees of subtlety; some of the possibilities are indicated by the student projects included in this issue. The creation of power structures is fundamentally to do with resources and their division. The role of the architect is to identify this allocation and then to recognise and exploit potential opportunities in the shaping of significant architecture. However, is the development of 'smart buildings' accompanied by the danger that one day our buildings will control us? In his new book Philip Kerr poses the question that perhaps the rise of these advanced building systems will lead to their controlling ourselves, so expressing the ultimate power of architecture over humanity, its originator.

Centre Georges Pompidou, Richard Rogers and Renzo Piano, Paris, 1977

THOMAS A MARKUS
WHAT DO BUILDINGS HAVE TO DO WITH POWER?

Things and words

In the myths of Australian Aboriginals the world was created by spirits of nature – human, animal and vegetable – in the 'Dreamtime'. The intimate link between people and nature is maintained by song, poetry, stories and painting. A Dreaming site is loaded with symbolic meaning, and these rituals keep the myth alive giving the site an invisible mental structure. That, rather than changes to its material form, make it significant. In other cultures this can be overlooked when space is shaped by buildings and settlements. These, by far the most important products of material cultures, are so concrete and rich, so obviously useful, that they can swamp the invisible structures which give meaning to both use and form, whether in the Australian bush or the European city.

Except for gibberish, language means something, but that buildings mean something is not a familiar idea. Of course a lot is clear. Someone has decided who can use a building. We share it with others and have little doubt whether it is a palace, a church or an electronics factory. Its form arouses feelings alongside the associations which spring from a Greek temple portico, a pointed spire, stainless steel tubes or explicit symbols such as an Imperial eagle, a Christian cross or an IBM logo. All this is part of the building's narrative, but we still find it hard to say that it means something, that there are invisible structures present.

That may be difficult with language too, but with buildings it seems much harder. The search for meaning entails a number of questions. What kinds of things do buildings mean? How do they do so? Do they have the same meanings for everyone? Do meanings change over time, even for a given person?

In language the inner and outer worlds meet. This is equally the case in buildings. This is so vital for understanding them that, despite many misleading links between buildings and language which have been made, it is useful to compare our task with the work of those whose concern is language itself.

Poets, philosophers, linguists, semioticians, psychoanalysts, literary critics and workers in artificial intelligence explore meanings behind what common sense tells us. But even their most hard fought battles, in what Eliot calls 'a raid on the inarticulate/With shabby equipment always

deteriorating',[1] rely on everyday use. Wittgenstein said that language means what its users take it to mean; artists and intellectuals share ordinary meanings with each other and with us. This is the secure anchor and salutary test of their work. There is no private language.

When the ordinary world is obscure and confused, digging beneath its surface is that much harder. This seems to have happened to towns and buildings as a result of an erosion which started some 200 years ago, a period which, paradoxically, defined itself in terms of making the world clear through reason. Designers, scholars, critics and users now no longer seem to inhabit the same world. Many places no longer distinguish clearly between public and private. A shopping mall is accessible to all and hence 'public' but feels as if someone controls it, and us, through a powerful presence. Ambiguity in forms, confusion about function, or labyrinthine space deprive towns and buildings of clarity. Forms have become difficult to decode. Classical buildings are as likely to be associated with 1930s European Fascism as with republicanism or humanism; the modern movement with democratic freedom as with doctrinaire bureaucracy. Jameson[2] argues that post-modernism has challenged the very notion of meaning with its jokes, disconn-ections, historical cannibalism and 'photorealism', and that its roots are in the free market of multinational capital.

Much of what is written about towns and buildings feels equally obscure, esoteric and alienating. Despite the writers sharing daily use of buildings with us, little seems to be shared in the way of responses and it is difficult to encroach into their territory. The obscurity of buildings and of the language about them are of course two sides of the same coin.

All this is sometimes defended as a mature tolerance for contradictions and layers of meaning, a view based on work such as Sennett's.[3] His defence of creative disorder depended, like Erikson's psychoanalytic theory of adolescence upon which it was based, on a tolerance of ambiguity and contradiction. It was the unexpected conflict, the hidden paradox, the surrealist jokes which were maturing. The argument was a vindication of creative disorder, slippages of meaning which illuminate the world, but not a defence for chaos in that world itself. More recently in a reaction to older, patriarchal order, which structuralism left unscathed, post structuralism, post-modernism and deconstruction have made the ambiguities of *montage* a targeted objective. The fracturing of things that are conventionally glued together has been specially powerful in drama, since Brecht. By dissociating words, gestures and facial expression the meaning of daily relations is probed. While this may work on the stage, and illuminate that which is offstage, if these dissociations were present in daily life then relations would lose all meaning. Similarly, if experiments in 'stage' architecture were transported to the street, then everyday experience would become bizarre and alienating and they would lose their significance.

Of course the media texts are more accessible. They identify visible and important issues. Some concern failures: technical ones of poor construction and shabby finishes, high energy consumption and ecological damage; or visual ones of inhuman scale, coldness, or even of disease (Prince Charles's 'carbuncle' metaphor has become a byword). In housing there is reference to vandalism, crime and lack of neighbourliness. Some concern successes – praise for key art galleries and museums, reverence for a historic heritage which combines the sacredness of cathedrals, the splendour of country mansions, the innocence of nature in the great estates, and the inventiveness of the industrial entrepreneur. These failures and successes are real enough and the media do open them to public debate. And yet their silence over less visible failings and successes and their blinkers, obstruct the quest for meaning. In advocating good modern design and rejecting timorous historical pastiche the distinction between the 'shock of the new' and loss of meaning is erased. Whatever the rights and wrongs of that, by squeezing out all issues other than those of form the debate is further trivialised. So it is good to stay close to language because it acts as a model for what it is like to go beneath the surface and behind silence.

. Language is at the core of making, using and understanding buildings. Through it a community articulates its feelings and thoughts about them, to share its experience of meaning. Much of what we think and feel is the direct outcome of descriptive texts – scholarly works, educational material, media productions, travel literature and exhibition catalogues. There is a host of prescriptive ones too such as competition conditions, briefs, legislation, building regulations, feasibility reports and design guides. These texts exist before a building is designed and yet in many ways 'design' it. Their language, like all language, cannot be innocent. The values and intentions of their authors are present in length, subdivision, tone, the degree of elaboration of parts and the things that are not said – the silent discourse – and above all the texts use everyday speech

categories. Classification puts these names for things, people, spaces and processes into an order. That buildings can be regarded as classifying devices is obvious in libraries where classification is overt and governs the location of books in space and the very structure of that space. But all buildings classify something.

The way the material and our inner world are related through language is so problematic that only a treatise in linguistics or philosophy can unravel it. As I am neither a linguist nor a philosopher I shall not attempt that, but its essence is simple enough and in setting it out I am indebted to one of the scholastic pioneers of material culture, Kouwenhoven.[4]

Every building is experienced as a concrete reality. I visit a bank. Behind its classical entrance are glass doors, its banking hall is domed and it has an elaborate mosaic floor. Across its mahogany counter I face a familiar clerk. I see doors to other rooms and other people behind the counter, but I do not recognise these spaces nor these people. The bank has its own smell and sounds. The entire experience is unique. By calling it a 'bank' I am using what Kouwenhoven calls something 'inherently "defective" . . . a sort of generalised, averaged out substitute for a complex reality comprising an infinite number of individual particularities'.[5] If I speak to someone whose sole experience is of the Hong Kong and Shanghai Bank's headquarters we are likely to misunderstand each other. If the hearer shares the experience of the speaker then the value of the spoken word is that it makes communication about myriads of experiences possible by means of a very limited vocabulary. However, 'words do not have meaning; they convey it. But they can convey it only if the receiving consciousness can complete the current of meaning by grounding it in comparable particulars of experience'.[6] Otherwise, though we exchange words we think we understand, the currents pass each other by like ships in the night. Of course the comparability might be quite remote or only metaphorical but, given the skills of a good novelist or poet, even such germs of shared experience are sufficient.

Kouwenhoven used this argument in relation to artefacts but it is equally applicable to buildings; when the particularity of experience is not shared, then what is said is not heard. When writers do not even try to base their abstractions on shared experience then, by Kouwenhoven's definition, they cannot make sense to anyone.

He aimed not to discredit language, but to warn that its very abstraction is its weakness. Short of remaining mute nothing can be done about that; but an awareness of this fragility is a strong motivation for holding tight to experience. In any case this shortcoming is exactly its power when it comes to analysis. We simply have no other way to deal with the invisible, mental structures. So where are we? We are concerned with buildings about which there are texts; that is, things and words (and I am adding more words). There are live debates about whether the meaning of a text (who 'writes' the text) is created by the author, or by the reader, and also about the degree to which both are socially formed. Some of these debates are profound; others, in Short's words are 'structuralist gibberish, about as digestible and intelligible as overcooked suet pudding'.[7] My position is unambiguous: just as meaning in language needs a speaker and a listener who are members of the same language using community, so buildings and their texts acquire meaning when the subject (an observer, user, reader) experiences a building or a text about it; when the two worlds intersect. Subject and object are embedded in – neither free of nor determined by – their historical societies. The first world is an outer, visible one (which is, of course, the result of its author's inner world) and the second an invisible, inner world. At this intersection the Cartesian boundary between object and subject dissolves. So our study of meaning will have to embrace three domains: the building, the text and the experiencing subject, all in a language using society. In practice I shall not be able to tackle all three in equal depth, but this map of the task suggests that power, my central theme, will permeate its every nook and cranny.

A case: If meaning springs from experience, what is it about buildings, texts and subjects that matters? The answer returns to the idea of an unfolding serial event, a building as a narrative. From the moment it is conceived, through its design, production, use, continuous reconstruction in response to changing use, until its final demolition, the building is a developing story, traces of which are always present.

In the seminal but indigestible work by Frankl[8] which we shall consider again, he cites a part of such a narrative – the case of a mediaeval monastery converted to a courthouse. This troubles him, as if it were an obstacle to understanding, an unfortunate accident, rather than the inevitable stuff of history. He argues that if some knowledge is missing then a building makes less sense than it might.

> If we study buildings of older cultures and find one lacking in original fittings because, for example, what was once a monastery is now a courthouse, then our need to know something becomes still more conspicuous. The spectator who is without knowledge has even greater need for the right reference when confronted by a building designed for an obsolete purpose . . . to reconstruct the essence of the building.[9]

Frankl contrasts this with experience in one's own time where, he says, problems can arise because whilst 'we understand without explanation the spaces created for . . . common purposes' we may lack the experience to cope with a new function 'for which . . . a person probably needs special instruction'.[10] Certainly for his example, a factory, this would be true for an art historian. Though the monastery-into-court is a dramatic metamorphosis of a kind for which the National Archives in Paris provide ample evidence chiefly as unexecuted, Revolutionary projects especially from the *Directoire* onwards in the 1790s, it is untypical, for change is normally far less abrupt.

Frankl's second example is misleading because he envisages no change in the factory. There is no stasis though, whether change is perceptible depends on the time intervals used. Material, fabric, use, the experience and perception of users and observers, and hence the things said and written about the building, change – minutely hour by hour, dramatically century by century. Whilst the transformations in the 'case' could never be governed entirely by the building and those who occupy it (such as changes in the Rule or structural weaknesses) the possibility for change depended on inherent material factors – space, load-bearing potential and location in the town as well as on some kind of analogy between spaces for liturgy and for legal processes. However, external factors, such as the abrupt political upheaval, are necessary too, otherwise 'desert island history' would be possible.

The ever-changing interplay between internal and external forces should be a major task for the architectural historian but the tradition is to treat the moment of a plan or photograph, and their accompanying text, as timeless. It was Frankl's achievement to break out of this idealist straight-jacket as far as forms were concerned, only to betray his insight by transferring to function the notions of 'essence'.

To bring the narrative to the present, let us suppose that the courthouse was used until the 19th century when the building was restored by Viollet-le-Duc and that it was abandoned until it was recently converted into a chamber music concert hall. Further, that there is historical material available: information on the first abbot and his community, their land holdings, patrons and political connections; drawings of the building as it was at the first conversion as well as of the new court arrangements; records of political debates in the two Chambers of the 1790s about the appropriation and utilisation of ecclesiastical property; an illustrated text as to model courts for the new *Tribuneaux*; a lawyer's account of its use; some scholarly articles as well as tourist literature; and the brief for the concert hall. These suppositions are not far-fetched; such a wealth of information, can be recovered for thousands of buildings.

Since the only experience I can know is my own this narrative now continues as a short piece of autobiography which is fictional, but only in a

Proposed layout for courts during the French Revolution

trivial sense. I want to be true to the narrative, that is to encompass its entire life from abbey church to the evening when I listened to a concert.

I see its exterior mass and detail in its setting on the edge of the place before it becomes dark and, in walking round it, I become familiar with the way its entrances, including the triple portail and its carved tympanum, are connected to and visible from the spaces outside. Inside it is now lit so that there are dramatic contrasts between the dark volumes of the vaulted mass and the strongly lit capitals, columns and sanctuary floor. I am able to wander around before the concert – from narthex into nave, to side chapels, transepts, the chevet and the lower crypt where the founding abbot lies buried. Both here and up above there are other tombs in the floor, walls and under canopies between columns.

My experience is of the location and general form of the building, the details of what is on its surfaces, its colour, the stories told by its carvings, the geometrical ornament. Some of the forms I can only guess at as they are in the dark. It is also of its current purpose – the musical performance which I will shortly share with the rest of the audience and the musicians. Further, I sense how its spaces are organised – I know what is near the entrance, what lies deep within, what is next to what, how all these spaces are connected.

Even before the concert I feel that I am in touch with a space ordered through contrasts of dark and light, mass and detail, solid and void. It has a movement, a progression, both forwards towards the place of action, and upwards into a dimly perceived space. The contrasts feel familiar as contradictions in my own life; the dimness as the ever present obscurity around my understanding of the world and myself in it; the dynamics of movement as metaphors for growth; the rhythm and order as a lively but familiar security. Inevitably the personal memories and images aroused mingle with those awakened by the guessed purposes of others who have been, or now are here; monks, judges, lawyers, witnesses, musicians, audiences. Soon, listening to the secular music played directly above the first abbot – 'founded on' him – I pick up an additional numinous sense besides its conventional meanings, one that was probably intended in deciding to play in the church. I am surrounded by tombs of its earlier inhabitants and patrons – a story evidently more ancient than the music. I connect the music, the brightly lit performing platform and the position of the conductor with such liturgical experience as I possess. On departure I purchase a short illustrated tourist guide. The direct experience has stopped.

During the following weeks I gain access to the printed and drawn record which connect the design with others of the same Order, in the political context of the time. I see the limitations on representation imposed by the Rule. I understand something of the wealth behind the building; the motivations of the aristocratic patrons who lie buried there; the reason why this particular master mason – recognisable from his moulding profiles – was imported. I grasp the transformation from church to court, the Republican notions of justice, and the meaning of the spatial layout and its furnishings to a working lawyer of the time. I see analogies between the position of the abbot's throne, in front of a crucifix, and the judge's chair in front of the *tricouleur,* between monks and clerical assistants, on the one hand, and lawyers and officials on the other; between lay worshippers in the nave and visitors in the public gallery of the lawcourt. The relations are validated in one case by the presence of the sacred and in the other by the State's justice. I ask in what ways the public rituals of these two hierarchical institutions, deriving their authority from an invisible being at their apex, are the same and in what ways different. One creates a community through shared bonds, and the other represents the processes of power; how can one space carry such different meanings? I begin to wonder about the tightness of fit between space and its meaning.

I learn something of the beliefs of mid-19th century conservationists which enabled them to create gross distortions in the name of historical veracity. I see in the brief for the concert hall something of today's idea of culture and especially clearly, here, its association with history and the sacred. This, for me, casts light on the role of cultural buildings, including also museums and art galleries, as today's sacred places. All these 'discoveries' are welded onto my own experience on that seminal evening.

This imaginary autobiographical 'case' is a skeleton without flesh. Indeed how could it ever be complete when there are many histories and layers of meaning? The building, what is written about it, and what is experienced form a seamless fabric. The richness is such that there is rarely an opportunity to develop any single case as completely as this one potentially is, but the 'case' serves its purpose.

Building and their texts as social practice

This seamless fabric stretches through real historical societies. To tease out its parts I want to represent this society-in-history as having three domains: social practices, social relations and subjects. Making buildings and writing texts about them are two particular social practices. So is the use of language, the most important practice of all. Subjects both constitute and are constituted by society, and in their social relations they discover the meanings of their practices.

The building
There were things to be seen – spaces with a geometry, and fabric with repre-

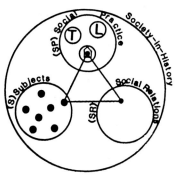

T = texts about buildings

L = language

⌂ = designing and producing buildings

Building and their texts as social practice

11

sentational and abstract ornament facing both inwards and outwards. The surfaces were articulated by openings, pilasters and ribs into subdivisions which were repeated rhythmically. Some had applied material – carpets, wall hangings or paintings. There were symbols, emblems and written inscriptions. The column clusters and mouldings were hierarchically ordered, a feature which Panofsky[11] has related to the logical structure of scholasticism. We saw window tracery, a heavily carved tympanum, column capitals and tomb carvings.

There were juxtapositions on, or substitutions for, earlier work; not only a sequence of mediaeval forms, but remnants of the neoclassical courtroom and, now, modern plate glass, furniture and lighting. In a 'style' these formal elements cohere. The classical system was eventually governed, to its last detail, by prescriptive rules – verbal and graphic – which from the 15th century onwards form the core of architectural texts. Forms tell an unbelievably rich narrative, both informative and moving. How informative and how moving depends on what intellectual and emotional equipment is brought along.

Some things we saw were more obviously to do with people. Some were people – playing or listening to music and selling programmes. We found or recovered evidence of earlier inhabitation and were able to imagine monks in the choir, priests at the altar (which has survived), layfolk in the nave, the judge, lawyers and witnesses in the space now occupied by the musicians and the courtroom public in the present auditorium.

There is no limit to what is recoverable about the purpose and organising principles of the liturgy, the monastic Rule or the legal process even down to the details of processions for particular feast days or procedures during particular trials.

For reasons adduced by Kouwenhoven, unless experience is shared the picture of function given by any text, no matter how elaborate, will remain on the surface. This becomes clear if we consider the meaning of sites which no amount of insight by a scholar, tourist or critic can fully capture. How would such a stranger feel about, or see, the seaside hotel of our childhood holidays? Reconstruction will be hard work and will at best produce a passable likeness, at worst a caricature. That is to say the rich narrative about use, whether observed, remembered or recovered, is as moving and poetic as that of form, despite the dry sound of 'function'.

In the 'case' we also became aware of spatial relations. Moving in through the narthex led to a sequence of spaces. Sometimes there was a single route, and to return we had to retrace our steps, sometimes there was an alternative. Some spaces were shallow, near the entrance, others deep, reached after passing through many intervening spaces. Some were barred by rules

signified by locked doors and signs. Each was for a recognisable purpose, and for identifiable persons. The picture we built up was one of 'nextness' – topological rather than geometrical – into which the entire functional description fitted; not only who did what, when and with whom, in what form of space, but where and next to whom.

So observation, experience, the texts and the drawings produced knowledge of form, function and space. In everyday life, these cohere seamlessly but for analysis of meaning it is useful to consider them as separate discourses. Of the three, form and space are permanent (unless material changes occur). Function is not – it is the social practice of use 'inscribed' into the building.

Some monastic communities had baroque buildings, lawcourts have been built in many styles and both can operate in a variety of spatial structures, each of which signifies a different social relation. In other words there is no immutable relation between form, function and space despite Sullivan's famous dictum 'form follows function'. They are independent and yet if it still makes sense to ask whether an entire building means something it looks as if we shall have to seek an answer in a common field which can tell us something about all its properties. That actually destroys the idea of a coherent, self-contained discourse such as 'architecture' is commonly held to be. So where shall we look?

The building came into being through the actions of owners, investors, designers, builders, craft workers, princes of the Church and State and legislators. To keep it in existence needs yet others such as cleaners. They, with all users, were knitted into their own historical societies. It therefore seems inescapable to take the social relations of all these people as that common field.

Before developing that idea we need to say something about the other social practice – the writing of texts – and about the subject.

The text Prescriptive texts are rare in the period of the monastic church, but become more frequent after the 17th century, starting as simple letters, becoming more elaborate Acts of the state, town council minutes, competition briefs, building legislation or design guides and finishing up as today's substantial design briefs.

The text has its own history. It appears in a place and time and in a specific form, and is produced, stored and distributed by such institutions as a monastic library, a publisher, a printer, a gallery, a university or a newspaper. Besides its words it may contain numbers, tables, drawings, photographs, computer simulations and soundtracks. It adopts conventions – styles – of writing, graphics, composition and reproduction.

Subject We know subjectivity from inside – this is familiar territory with its many layered onion-like meanings. We know that this is a less tangible entity than the building or the text. Though I make no attempt to offer tools for its analysis, the subject enters the argument.

At the risk of becoming boring, it is necessary to repeat that subjects are also in society-in-history. The critic, scholar or analyst is merely another subject, despite the brilliance of their critiques, the weight of their tomes, or learnedness of their theses. They are products of their personal histories, they view the evidence through their own spectacles. The 'case' was useful if for nothing else than to illustrate that there is no way of standing outside; as interpreter I was inside the narrative I was interpreting. It may be humbling but it is as well to be clear about it.

If meaning is in society-in-history we face two forms of a troublesome contradiction which has been hugely debated. One is that between the individual and society. Is the individual nothing more than the social product of genetic, environmental and economic forces? Or are there some traits which are 'essential' to being human, something we can call human 'nature' which is prior to and beyond the reach of socialisation? The other is between material artefacts like buildings and texts, and especially works of art, and society. Are these reducible to social formation through their authors' history, or is there something 'essential', universal, which elicits the 'aha!' response?

To give an answer to the first question which feels authentic I want to distinguish between two kinds of human relations. The first depends on roles, structures and control of resources. These constitute an individual through social forces of power relations. For the second I rely in part on phenomenology and on Husserl's notion of the 'lifeworld'[12] – a world in which I experience myself and to which I belong, through my body. I form relations, which Gorz[13] calls 'bonds', beyond and in some way the opposites of socially constituted ones. Though developing in and through the selfsame societies, attachment to others by these bonds are not determined by social forces of power relations. Gorz uses maternal love as the outstanding example ' . . . by its essence a threat to any order'.[14] Although these bonds are free of the constraints which determine power relations, they can only grow and be experienced within a concrete social setting. He could have extended this example to include all kinds of love, friendships and solidarity.

The reality of this inner world cannot be reached from outside-in. 'It is impossible to exteriorise interiority, or objectivise the subjective'[15] but this does not require us to believe in a prior 'nature' outside history. It is in that history, and only there, that each individual's inner world is formed, by being in touch with elements of nature – our own bodies, seasons, weather, living plants and creatures, food, and other materials, sometimes raw, sometimes highly processed by a technological culture – and above all with others, including others' bodies. This is so much what being human is about, that it seems legitimate to speak of it as human 'nature'. Evolution and genetic inheritance, childhood environment and specific local culture are all formative, as they are in the ability to learn a language. Even a history that stretches back into evolutionary origins and is common to all, forms me in a unique way. I have a body, like everyone else, but the way I feel in it, the way I use it, say in a dance or in a sexual relation, is unique to me. Again, like all human beings, I have the ability to speak languages. But I use the specific language of the community to which I belong and I say things that I alone think and feel. No one else can say exactly the same things now or ever again.

It is easier to grasp the uniqueness of every person's 'lifeworld' when ancient and shared continuities are in some marked way disrupted by a moment of history. A word, smell or shape may then carry a meaning of destruction, despite it being generally a sign of healing. In architecture, after two thousand years of classical order, Mussolini's use of classicism may have wiped out the harmony of the Pazzi Chapel for a whole generation. Such disruptions shape both the socially constituted power relations and the bonds which spring from the inner 'lifeworld'; just as the individual is more than just a socially constituted creature, so society is more than a mere aggregate of its individual members.

This points to an answer to the second question. If created objects have 'essence' this originates with the 'nature' of the creator who is both constituted by and formed within society. Social analysis can explain the qualities of this object, but it will not explain it away. Here is history's dual presence again, and in so far as the object has meanings deriving from human 'nature' it will evoke an 'aha!' from others, unless a Mussolini-like event has wiped out that possibility.

Buildings are the concrete setting for both kinds of relations, but they are more than passive containers. Like all practices they are formative, as much through the things that happen in them, their functional programme, as by their spatial relations and their form. My position then is that I pay the utmost respect to material history and the social relationships it creates, in particular to bodies in buildings space. Without that history nothing makes sense, but even with it there remain meanings which are intractable to outside-in analysis. Here I have to rely on my own experience and hope that I share enough with others for it to be communicable in words.

Just what is the role of mind, consciousness and language in this world of bodies in space, of buildings as material containers, I have to leave to philosophers to explain.

Tools of analysis A number of the analytical approaches are familiar and straightforward, though even they prompt questions. Others, however, are less so and need to be described.

The building – Form It seems hardly necessary to say that the form of the church-court-house-concert hall produces a powerful experience but this is not the only relevant factor. We must also consider the tradition of historical scholarship, criticism, teaching and the media which treats form as the defining quality of architecture. Most of the analytical tools have their origins in art scholarship. They examine stylistic development, articulation, iconography and perception in an unbroken tradition from the Renaissance to German idealist scholarship of the last century.

There is a huge body of material available for analyses of form: drawings, texts, archaeological and architectural surveys, photographs and models. Little of it has been used for social interpretation and yet even historians for whom architecture has been an autonomous art form have recently acknowledged that its meaning may reside in society. Summerson[16] concludes that the language of classicism relates to ' . . . the whole question of architecture as a vehicle for social meaning'. Watkin[17] in his review of how architectural history is done, notes that one of its most 'striking recent characteristics is . . . the increasingly determined attempt to relate buildings to the society in which they were produced', though he is pessimistic about such attempts.

For Frankl[18] form has three components. First, spatial composition – the geometry of space. The medium is the plan and his analysis of that became the inspiration for Kaufmann[19] in his work on the 'revolutionary' architects of the late 18th century, and for Giedion[20] on the Baroque. Second, he analyses mass and surface by techniques based on those which Wölfflin used for the Renaissance and Baroque. He might have called this concrete material 'physiognomy' but prefers 'corporeality'. Third, he considers the effects of light, colour and other optical phenomena, creating changing images with every viewpoint which coalesce in the mind into a single sensation, a view clearly derived from the then new Gestalt psychology.

These three combine with function to give meanings about the world. For instance the contrast between the Renaissance and the Baroque Frankl[21] describes as 'finite' against 'infinite'; 'microcosm' against 'macrocosm'; and 'a complete, closed, self-sufficient unit' against 'a fragment that opens to the universe because it is incomplete'. These meanings were intended by the designers and are evoked for everyone who experiences the building. This message is universal in two senses: it is about the universe and its meaning will persist for all time, for everyone.

Amongst the most powerful challenges to the view of forms as metaphors are those derived from Saussure. The idea of a sign as an arbitrary combination of a form (signifier) and an idea (signified) – the combination being created both in its generation (utterance) and in its reception (hearing/reading) through codes – has been applied to architecture. Eco[22] treats formal elements as parts of a sign system which is interpreted through a code.

Eco[23] distinguishes between various signs denoting construction or use. For each there is a word, such as 'dome' or 'staircase'. By extension if a form has no constructional or functional purpose, there is no unambiguous word for it. Language cannot cope with such forms which, hence, are impossible to understand. They might even be invisible. The names for the parts of the classical system, even if the forms are rooted in primitive history, were needed not only to write the prescriptive rules, but also to see them. One of the most disorientating aspects of recent architecture is that some of its spatial and formal inventions are not nameable.

Such approaches allow new evidence about the form-function link to be used. They make it worthwhile to speculate, for instance, on the shift from Classical to Tudor in schools, on the role of Scottish baronial in Robert Adam's Edinburgh prison and on the meaning of the Crystal Palaces 'high-technology' forms. But though semiotics may provide some insights, it fails to explain how choices are made. What is the effect of dominant groups – civil, military, ecclesiastical or, say Freemasonic? Whose formal codes emerge? What explains exclusions – censored forms? And when forms are driven by technology, what explains technological censorship? Why did even semiotics remain stuck in the formalist groove?

Function The functions of monastic liturgy, Revolutionary justice, and a modern musical production speak about society. The abstract, socially-formed language oppositions 'sacred-secular', 'lawful-criminal', and 'professional-lay' became concrete in spaces and in their labels which often stand for both space and use; 'choir' and 'lawcourt' are both places and institutions.

Though the labels encapsulate all the evidence – from use, observation and texts – Frankl[24] recognised the difficulty of reconstructing the functional narrative. Briefs, if they ever existed, have often disappeared without trace and there are few records of spoken instructions. Functional prescriptions are being continuously rewritten, and what survives may be in ephemeral texts such as account books or minutes of meetings.

Once a new function is named its ambiguity disappears. Its name affects the choice of designer, how the building is financed, its location, Strong labels establish an identity between place

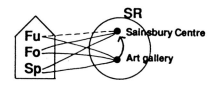

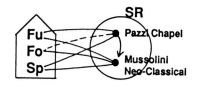

FROM ABOVE: Sainsbury Centre spatial relationships; Pazzi Chapel Spatial relationships

and activity; by the end of the 18th century this had happened for 'school' but not for the 'Sunday school'. Today 'supermarket' has achieved it but 'health club' has not yet done so.

The massive civic building programme of the First Empire, which Teysott[25] has quantified, was partly achieved by conversion for instance of churches into prisons, barracks and lawcourts. The extent to which a switch of label (function) is strong enough to obliterate established meanings depends on whether there is a new conjunction with form and space at a new point in the domain of social relations. Thus the Sainsbury Centre, with its supermarket shed form and space, and its 'art gallery' label, shifts the meaning of the art gallery in terms of social relations. A new type has come into being. If the points refuse to converge – if one simply cannot accept a formal or spatial solution to a given function – then there is a contradiction of meaning in the material world as in the case of Mussolini's classicism.

Once the material is assembled, its analysis starts from a set of questions. In the instance of the monastery converted to a courthouse who defined the first function? Who, and by what authority, transformed it? What physical changes were needed? Who named the functions? And what does it mean if a building designed for the first function was able to be used for the second?

Space Lefebvre's[26] analysis of space as a social production has connected abstract space in science, social space and concrete, material space. To push the analysis of spatial experience further the space syntax method of Hillier and Hanson[27] – who represent spatial structures by the standard method of graphs – is more suitable. They produced a family of quantified measures, to describe and analyse spatial configuration.

Underlying such techniques are some basic assumptions. First, that from amongst the strangers outside, buildings admit two categories – 'inhabitants' and 'visitors'. The former have an investment of power and are the controllers, the latter enter as subjects of the system – the controlled shoppers, diners, museum visitors, inmates in hospitals and prisons (where a 'visit' may be of several years' duration), theatre audiences and church congregations. The building's *raison d'être* is to interface the two groups and exclude strangers. Second, that it is the same thing which explains both society and space – social relations. Society's organisation can be described in the abstract but in the material world it is space that does so. There is no aspatial society and no asocial space. Third, (following Durkheim) that social organisation is of two kinds: organic solidarity and mechanical solidarity. The former consists of mutually interdependent relations where everyone has a role. It is often highly structured and hierarchical and

needs to be articulated in space. Businesses and hospitals are typical. The latter is the relation between people who share beliefs. Members of a community of scholars, a church or a political party have a mechanical solidarity. It often has no programmed spatial requirements – it is transspatial (but not aspatial). People participate in both kinds of relation – a nurse may also belong to a church, or a factory worker to a trade union.

Hillier and Hanson,[28] illustrate four formally identical plans differing only in the number of entrances and interconnections between spaces. Each is represented by a circle (the outside by a cross in a circle) and each permeable link by a line. The resulting graphs have been 'justified' on the spatial maps by placing the spaces on a series of lines, starting with a space on line zero, (in this example the outside space). Those one step from this are placed on line one, those two steps away on line two and so on. The depth of all the spaces from the starting point is immediately evident; as is the presence of branching trees or looping rings. Spaces lying on the former have no alternative routes to them, whereas those lying on a ring are on at least two routes.

The spatial maps are very different. Some are shallow, some deep, some 'ringy', some tree-like. Two spaces A and B in identical relation to a third, C, are said to be 'symmetrical' with respect to C. If their spatial distances from C are different, they are 'asymmetrical'. The total amount of asymmetry from any point relates to its mean depth measured by its 'relative asymmetry' (RA), the values ranging from zero (low) to one (high). Each space is a number of steps from all others; those that are, in sum, spatially closest to them all (low RA) are the most integrated. They characteristically have dense traffic through them. Those that are furthest (high RA) are the most segregated – often for privacy, or reserved for ceremonial functions.

Where spaces have more complex forms than these simple rectangles – for instance L-shapes – techniques are available for breaking them down into their elementary forms without re-entrant angles ('convex' shapes).

In public buildings there is a shallow visitor zone. Visitors interface with the inhabitants at some spatial barrier which prevents deeper penetration: the counter in shops and banks, the bar in pubs, the proscenium arch in theatres, the gallery space of museums. The inhabitants occupy a zone beyond this which, to the visitors, looks deep and usually has its own access. Depth indicates power. The bank manager is deeper than the clerks, and the consultant deeper than the nurse. The person with the greatest power is at the tip of a tree, reached through corridors, stairs, outer and inner offices and waiting lobbies.

The relation between spatial structure and function is loose. One model of medical practice creates deep, tree-like clinics, where patients

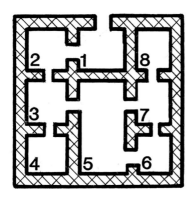

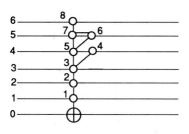

	Depth	RA
⊕	0	0.786
1	1	0.536
2	2	0.357
3	3	0.250
4	4	0.500
5	4	0.286
6	5	0.464
7	5	0.429
8	6	0.571
Mean	3.750	0.464

FROM ABOVE: Floor plan, spatial map and RA value

15

meet doctors only in the consulting room beyond which is a deeper zone invisible to the patients, with its own entrance and circulation, designed to maintain a certain magic and to reinforce professional power. Another model results in a shallow, 'ringy' structure with shared entrances and circulation routes, less control by reception spaces and some solidarity which spans across the doctor-patient gap.

In one kind of building, argue Hillier and Hanson, the normal relationship is inverted. The visitors are deep within, increasing depth signifying decreasing power, and the inhabitants in a shallow, often 'ringy', zone at the surface controlling access to the deeper parts. These are institutions – the prisons, hospitals and asylums.

An example illustrates this. Robert Adam's fourth design, based on Bentham's Panopticon, for the Edinburgh Bridewell (1791) shows that the prisoners, in cells at the periphery of the half drum, have access to outside exercise yards. The cells and the yards are under surveillance from two separate observation towers. The first (1) is clearly at the end of a shallow sequence of gate, entrance lobby, governor's garden, offices and house, but the second (13) appears to be deep in the plan, not where inhabitants are supposed to be. At basement level a tunnel connects the two. The spatial map shows that this brings space (13) to the surface, only one step from space (1), so that it is located in the shallow outer zone. Visibility links are shown by dotted lines. The overlaying of permeability and visibility defines surveillance.

Bridges and galleries, like the Bridewell tunnel, achieve topological adjacency which is impossible on one plane. Besides giving increased control as at Edinburgh, they can impose strict limits on the spaces used by the visitors. The tubes through which passengers in the Charles de Gaulle airport in Paris are moved between specific inlet and outlet points across the open central hall are such a device. The apparent freedom of the plan is negated by a transparent straightjacket. The contradiction is between an expectation aroused by form and the spatial reality.

The text The role of language in functional classification and typology has been discussed, but there are more general points to be made. Although prescriptive texts were quite abbreviated up to the 18th century, the richness of language about space more than compensated for this. Space became a metaphor for social relations. Bender [29] sees Defoe's description of London and especially the extraction of victims of the Great Plague from their shuttered houses into special plague houses, as part of the general move towards orderly segregation, surveillance and control which prefigured the vast penitentiary. Fielding's *Jonathan Wild* explores the power of the written record. Under the pose of public benefac-

tor Wild earns a vast fortune as a fence of stolen property and by using his sophisticated written index collects bounties for successfully bringing criminals to book. It is just such a record of past crime that Fielding the magistrate proposed to combine with a vast classified prison to be a model city of good order, where correction of the body went hand in hand with correction of the mind. Varey's [30] study of Defoe, Fielding and Richardson shows how space, whether of Robinson Crusoe's desert island or Clarissa's chamber, is a metaphor for changing property relations, domination by breaking down privacy (in Clarissa's case leading ultimately to her rape) and social control.

Language like this was disappearing. The loss was symmetrical. The texts about society become aspatial and those about buildings became asocial. As technical or artistic matters became separated from social issues, the very consciousness of buildings became thinner.

Prescriptions are not always written texts. Savignant's [31] study of drawing techniques traces verbal (*parole*) and graphic representation of buildings to two different traditions. The former is that of the intellectual and scientist working with abstractions; the latter that of the practical craftsman and builder, working with concrete material. The development of drawings into elaborate artistic creations marks a loss of control by architects over the functional programme, which was taken over by scientists, politicians and intellectuals. Architects were reduced to dressing up (*habillage*) of the forms demanded by others' rational-functional briefs. The drawing became as remote from life as did the text.

However, prescriptive drawings work in reverse by adding covert symbolic statements where overt verbal ones might be unacceptable. The report *Dwellings for the Working Classes* [32] lavishly illustrated a range of plans to solve the post-war shortage, where the kitchens (a word that appears nowhere in the text) and sculleries are often adjacent to the bath, copper and wash-house. Unlike the text, the plans make explicit the role of women as manual workers in what is called the 'domestic workroom'.

Design guides prescribe not for a building but for a type. They originate in the type plans described by Alberti and the Renaissance authors, and draw in treatises such as Blondel's *Cours* [33] and Durand's *Précis* [34]. Durand's *Recueil* [35] was an important contribution to the other tradition in illustrated prescription – that which uses existing specimens as exemplars.

Graphic 'texts' classify things just as do written ones and specifications, computer programs and Bills of Quantities by rules used for deciding similarity and dissimilarity. Language classifications encapsulate power structures, ideas, practices and beliefs. It is reasonable to regard

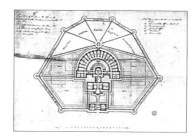

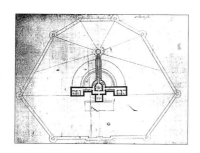

Robert Adam's fourth design for the Edinburgh Bridewell 1791, grand floor and basement plans

buildings as material classifying devices; they organise people, things and ideas in space so as to make conceptual systems concrete. The classes are established in the texts. For many tasks a durable taxonomy is a *sine qua non* because a large number of people or objects have to be arranged into classes and disposed in space in accordance with a social practice based on a theory. The division of children into classes according to age, gender, level of attainment or subject of study, and their location in 'classrooms' according to pedagogic rules, is an overt statement of educational philosophy. The classification of patients and the relation of their spaces to those of hospital staff translates medical theory into practice; whilst the arrangement of art or museum objects is a spatial mapping of artistic or scientific theory.

Such theories are implicit in briefs. The 1970 competition brief for Glasgow's Burrell Gallery determined basic features which each of the 242 entries possessed. This brief was represented in visual form, with each section and its subdivisions shown at a different level according to the hierarchy of headings, sub-headings and paragraphs. At each level the volume of text is represented by the area of a block. It is clear at a glance that some sections not only penetrate deeper, but are larger than others. Length and depth of text are measures of elaboration and crude indicators of emphasis. Three sections reach to the deepest level.

A8 sets out how designs are disqualified if they fail to meet other requirements of the brief. This is the 'gate' which operates as a meta-brief.

B3 spells out the rights of the Trustees and other parties. The power of Burrell the collector is enshrined in legal form. It was to be made concrete by another requirement – that the main rooms of his home, Hutton Castle in Berwickshire, be reproduced. At the heart of the plan these three rooms present the essence of the founder's home, furnished as they had been in the Castle. In one powerful gesture they speak of the person, his idea of art and his wealth. Here visitors speak in awed whispers. Above all, these rooms raise the history of the man, his collection and his home over the history of the objects which he collected from the immense space of the Far East, Near East and Europe over a time span ranging from pre-history to the 20th century. The choices were arbitrary and opportunistic. No place or time is essential. History, with the exception of the collector's own, became a pastime.

The only other part of the brief which descends to the deepest level are expansions of certain sections of European art, under C – Schedule of Accommodation. Despite the richness and splendour of the Chinese pottery and eastern carpets only the domestic product can be discriminated sufficiently to deserve this extra layer.

Text and diagram can combine into a spectacular prescription. William Stark's (1807) design for the Glasgow Lunatic Asylum was based on a brief which classified the patients by gender (men and women), economic class ('higher' and 'lower' rank – those who could pay and paupers) and medical condition ('Frantic', 'Incurable', 'Convalescent' and 'In an ordinary state'). These 16 classes appear in the left of a diagram. The symmetrical right half locates each at a specified distance from the centre and a specified storey height. Class was directly mapped in space and form.

In London's Natural History Museum some years ago a battle raged between adherents to two variants of evolutionary theory. The exact placing of key specimens was so crucial that some curators risked their jobs by illicitly changing their location at night, in an attempt to subvert the official theoretical position.

Social relations as meanings A variety of tools has been suggested for discovering the meaning of both text and building. If they are used, what kinds of meanings can we expect to find?

Buildings house bodies in space doing purposeful things; engaged in material processes. Taking part in a liturgical act, a legal trial or a concert is to be an actor in a material process. However, this inadequate description would fail to capture what is really going on were it not for the fact that 'liturgy', 'trial' and 'concert' are shorthands for events loaded with meaning. They tell us about whole sets of actors, responsibilities and power structures. They denote religious belief and practice, abstract concepts of justice, and the skill in making, as well as the experience of listening to, music. That is they describe social relations which I have already described as being of two kinds – those of power and those of bonds. These exist at the level of self to self, self to others and self to Other. For Marx exploitative production methods resulted in alienation at each of these three levels – from self, from others and from nature (an 'Other' with material evidence for its existence, and hence admissible within a materialist perspective).

Power has to do ultimately with resources. How these are divided becomes evident in hierarchical structures, control, surveillance, decision processes and in differential consumption. The monastic community had its structure. Inside the monastery church the roles of its members was signified by spatial location and by differences in the amount of space allocated, in the elaboration of furnishings, in seeing and being seen, and in entrances and circulation routes. At the apex of the pyramid was the abbot, deriving authority from the external relation of church and state and ultimately from an invisible presence signified by iconographic signs. The location and design of the tombs continued these relationships beyond death. Closeness to the heart of things – the altar

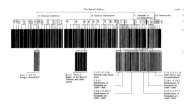

General View of the Plan of Classification, and of the Distribution of the Classes in the GLASGOW LUNATIC ASYLUM.

FROM ABOVE: The structure of the brief for the Burrell Gallery, 1970; classifications and spatial prescription for the Glasgow lunatic asylum, 1807

– was one important sign for both the living and the dead.

The most controlled members of a monastic community were the sick and the young. The plan of the ninth century monastery of St Gall fixes their lowly position. The infirmary and school are in the deepest part of the spatial structure, aligned with, and symmetrically disposed on either side of, the cosmic axis of the abbey church. Each of these two small cloisters has its own focal altar astride the same axis.

In the courthouse analogous features define the entire legal process: the judge at the apex, the state giving him authority in the name of invisible Justice which is signified in formal, functional and spatial features.

In the concert hall there is no doubt about the roles of conductor, players, organisers and audience. They are clear even to the uninitiated. The validation and resourcing of such cultural productions is however not evident from the building; this, ultimate, source of power is revealed by printed materials (programme notes, tickets and posters) and by general knowledge about culture which is shared by performers and audience. This power originates outside, as does the power of the church and the legal system, and it is trans-spatial.

That source determines how the concert hall, or any building, comes into being. Someone controls the necessary resources – land, raw materials, products, tools, machines and labour, or money to purchase them.

Possession of resources is power so it also purchases the freedom to appoint designers, set the terms of their employment, write the brief and select competition judges. The same groups create the rules by which the building is managed. They are formative in making building legislation, in the education of the professionals and in the provision of their institutions. The brief will be couched in their language; for scholars, critics and publishers they define another, the language of art criticism and art history – which treats buildings as large pieces of public sculpture – or of technology. Both these discourse fail to treat buildings as social objects.

Due to the inevitable link between resources and power, and their highly asymmetrical distribution, to build means to create asymmetries. The moral critique of society and its buildings is justice which can measure the degree of equity in the distribution of resources and power.

However, it is not as simple as that. Groups compete for power. There are counter- and sub-cultures, conflicts and shifts in its distribution. There will be 'subversive' elements in the practice of professionals and scholars. This complexity is present in buildings and their texts. A critique in terms of power has to be based on an analysis which takes this complexity on board. Some

meanings are quite obvious; others, as our 'case' showed, have to be teased out.

The forms are not autonomous; tracing their origins in patronage, education and the published texts, far from explaining them away or diminishing their emotional impact, will disclose a lot that enriches experience. Beyond what I have just said about monasteries, lawcourts and concerts there is no need to elaborate here how power is visible in functions.

In space, relations of power are ever-present. Depth, asymmetries and tree-like or 'ringy' forms control interfaces between people, and between them and objects such as museum exhibits. Hillier and Hanson[36] have shown how the conversion of Victorian working class housing by today's middle class involves little change in visible forms. The estate agents' brochures will pick up double glazing and central heating but not the transformation of space by the creation of new permeabilities and elimination of old ones by opening up and blocking off doorways. If space is mentioned it is in terms of technical improvement, status or convenience, but both parties instinctively know how it creates new interfaces between the household and its visitors, and new family relations in terms of childcare or housework.

Though power is so clear in all these formal, functional and spatial strategies, the other kind of relation, of bonds, always accompanies it. As Gorz[37] implies, it is its exact opposite though, strangely, instead of being about distributing finite resources – cake slicing – the stronger the identity of the self, or the relationship between two people or within a group, the more there is to share. In personal relationships it is called love or friendship and we look to poets or theologians to speak of it. In politics it is called solidarity. It is paradoxical in another way too. For whilst it ties people by a unity of interest, it liberates. These relations survive, even flourish, in the most oppressive situations; the struggle for justice generates bonds.

Such ideas are not abstractions. They are crucial for building design. Besides materialising through the life of the body, the chief way in which power and bond relations are made concrete is through bodies in space; in the space of buildings and towns.

We have looked at those things about buildings which make power concrete. It is the same things (there are no others) which express, give room for, sustain, deny or produce bond relations. Images can symbolise them. Function can be based on open-ended, easy to redefine briefs and rules which accommodate changing roles and activities as the spirit moves the occupants, with neither organisational nor material barriers. Spaces can be so linked that communication is free and frequent, making possible dense encounters between classes, groups and individuals. These are the basis for community, friendship and

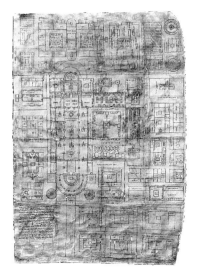

Ninth-century plan of the monastery of St Gall

solidarity. The alternative is controlled movement, under surveillance, for narrowly specified purposes. A place can be designed for discovery of both the self and others.

So in reality buildings always have double meanings in making concrete both power and bonds. Any building which satisfied the deepest longings for both justice and the creation of bonds would be a 'heavenly mansion'. It would house the structureless, powerless societies envisaged by both Marxists and Christians in visions so central to the Western tradition; a place for a community of love where State, class, marriage, the Church and all human institutions had withered away, to make possible totally just and unalienated relations. This vision inspired Utopian writers and designers. Both strands, the just society and the loving community, are present in their work. Thomas More set the pattern for the first and William Morris' (1891) *News from Nowhere* is the most lucid expression of the second.

Primo Levi's[38] profound observation of life in a dystopia, Auschwitz, is evidence of how people can always form bond relations, subverting even the most oppressive institutions and their buildings. One might then be tempted to say that this project of searching for meanings, with all its attendant practical and theoretical difficulties, does not really matter.

Before giving way to that temptation it is worth taking a closer look. The entrance gates announce 'Freedom through work' a startling restatement of the ideology of the Industrial Revolution. In reality production here was not just associated with disease, deformity and early death; death itself was its goal. For all the world this looked like a pavilion hospital. The contradiction between the rhetoric of the gate and the hospital plan on the one hand and the reality of the process on the other has other architectural analogues. As illustrated earlier the contradiction between freedom and constraint in the tunnels penetrating into open space at Charles de Gaulle airport. The most shattering experience is when the contradiction is between function and the agonising beauty of a city or building.

One way of reading Levi is indeed that bonds are independent of oppressive power structures, but that would be a terrible mistake. What he describes is the incalculable price which had to be paid for the creation of bonds in a system which used buildings as a key instrument of power. To a degree all pay a price in their daily built environment. That is the true measure of the interdependence of buildings and relations, and a good reason for pursuing the search for meaning in buildings.

Notes

1 TS Eliot, *Four Quartets*, Faber and Faber, London, 1944.
2 F Jameson, *Post-Modernism the Cultural Logic of Late Capitalism*, Verso, London, 1990.
3 R Sennett, *The Uses Disorder: Personal Identity and City Life*, Penguin Press, Harmondsworth, 1971.
4 JAK Kouwenhoven, 'American Studies: Words and Things', *Material Culture in America*, TJ Schlereth (Ed), American Association for State and Local History, Nashville, 1982, pp79-92.
5 *Ibid*, p83.
6 *Ibid*, p84.
7 JR Short, *Imagined Country: Society Culture and Environment*, Routledge, London, 1991, p224
8 P Frankl, *Principles of Architectural History: the Four Phases of Architectural Style, 1420-1900*, transl JF O'Gorman, MIT Press, Cambridge, Mass, 1914 (1969).
9 *Ibid*, p158.
10 *Ibid*, p158.
11 E Panofsky, *Gothic Architecture and Scholasticism*, Thames and Hudson, London, 1957.
12 S Husserl, *The Crisis of European Sciences and Transcendental Phenomenology*, translated D Carr, Northwestern University Press, Evanston, Illinois, 1970.
13 A Gorz, *Critique of Economic Reason*, transl G Handiside and C Turner, Verso, London, 1989.
14 *Ibid*, p175.
15 *Ibid*, p176.
16 J Summerson, *The Classical Language of Architecture*, Thames and Hudson, London, 1980, p114.
17 D Watkin, *The Rise of Architectural History*, The Architectural Press, London, 1980, p183.
18 P Frankl, *op cit.*
19 E Kaufmann, *Architecture in the Age of Reason*, Dover Publications, New York, rpt 1968.
20 S Giedion, *Space, Time and Architecture*, Harvard University Press, Cambridge, Mass, 1944.
21 P Frankl, *op cit.*
22 U Eco, 'Function and Sign: Semiotics of Architecture', M Gottdiener and A P Lagopoulos (eds), *The City and the Sign: an Introduction to Urban Semiotics*, Columbia University Press, New York, 1969 (1986), pp55-86.
23 *Ibid.*
24 P Frankl, *op cit.*
25 G Teysott, 'Citta-Servizi', *Casabella*, 424, pp56-65.
26 H Lefebvre, *Production of Space*, transl D Nicholson-Smith, Blackwell, Oxford, 1991.
27 B Hillier and J Hanson, *The Social Logic of Space*, Cambridge University Press, Cambridge, 1984.
28 *Ibid.*
29 J Bender, *Imaging the Penitentiary*, University of Chicago Press, Chicago, 1987.
30 S Varey, *Space and the Eighteenth Century English Novel*, Cambridge University Press, Cambridge, 1990.
31 J-M Savignant, *Dessin et Architecture du Moyen-Age au XVIIIᵉ Siècle*, École Nationale Supérieure des Beaux-Arts, Paris.
32 *Dwellings for the Working Classes*, HMSO, London, 1918.
33 J-F Blondel, *Cours d'architecture*, Paris, 1771-7.
34 J-N-L Durand, *Précis de Leçons d'Architecture Données à L'École Polytechnique*, Paris, 1802-9.
35 J-N-L Durand, *Recueil et Parallèle des Édifices de tous Genres, Anciens et Modernes*, Paris, 1801.
36 B Hillier and J Hanson, *op cit.*
37 A Gorz, *op cit.*
38 P Levi, *If This is a Man*, transl S Woolf, New English Library, London, 1962.

Auschwitz entrance gate

CHARLES JENCKS
APHORISMS ON POWER

For some reason, when I think about power I think aphoristically. Perhaps this is due to the famous saying of Lord Acton 'power tends to corrupt, and absolute power corrupts absolutely. Great men are almost always bad men' – which has led to so many further aphorisms, such as Adlai Stevenson's: 'power corrupts, but lack of power corrupts absolutely'. An interesting double truth: too much or too little power debases people which means that God must have meant everyone to have some power; that it should be decentralised in a network of reciprocal relations.

Once, when I was standing next to Philip Johnson, looking out of the window from the 52nd floor of the Seagram Building, surveying Manhattan as if it were a chessboard for his architectural play, I sensed the definite feelings of power an architect has in manipulating the environment, and treating it as his personal creation. At one point we had been talking about Albert Speer, and Philip said what a good American skyscraper architect Speer would have made. At another point, after showing me ten or so skyscrapers he was working on, he received a telephone call from Donald Trump, the developer-mogul, who then cancelled the design for 'Trump Castle', yet another pastiche skyscraper. Johnson was very angry and full of contempt for Trump, as if this upstart did not appreciate the symbolic importance and grandeur of a design by Johnson. As Johnson surveyed his Manhattan kingdom, looking out at the AT&T, the site of his Lipstick Building to come, and as his eyes narrowed with intensity, I couldn't help thinking: 'power concentrates the mind, and absolute power concentrates the mind absolutely'. In his case power-broking, manipulating architectural culture and creativity, is his form of power.

Later, I asked one of Johnson's understudies, the successful cosmopolite Robert Stern, 'what is this ambiguous thing, architectural power?' He professed not to know, but again returned to Acton and aphorism: 'power corrupts and architectural power corrupts architecture'. An interesting idea – too much architectural power in the hands of large corporations, an individual, or bodies like the old GLC, which had over a 1,000 architects working for it, destroys good architecture. Johnson's office,

at its height, had over a 100; Stern's, I believe, did also, and I can remember Sir Richard Rogers saying that he didn't want his firm to grow over 39, a wish that was soon proved wrong. Few, if any, architects can resist the pressure for more and bigger jobs and this, if Acton and Stern are right, will lead to corrupt architecture. Small is beautiful, big is boring; the clichés and aphorisms are usually right. However, sometime they are wrong, and it would be an interesting study to where and when Koolhaas, Pelli, Rogers, Piano and Foster sometimes kill the giant of boredom. For me IM Pei – on airplane magazines the most powerful global architect – never wins, but then my tastes on this matter are minority ones.

Peter Eisenman, who I also asked, said that Philip Johnson had more architectural power than any architect since Bernini, who worked for Popes and, unsuccessfully, for Louis XIV. Eisenman is another understudy of Johnson and he, like Stern, hopes to inherit the mantle as 'America's greatest power-broking architect', an unofficial title that magazines such as *Spy* and *Vanity Fair* regularly confer on someone or other. The idea is that there must be someone who has architectural power, so look around and find the most famous, rich, amusing, well-connected, successful architect . . . and who else but Philip. This is flattering for him, and he works very hard at brokering the latest style, and raising up the youngest-new thing: Moss today, Gehry yesterday, Eisenman, Graves and Stern the day before, Paul Rudolph and Louis Kahn the day before that.

Johnson has been crowning American architects, or playing John the Baptist to their Christ, since the late 1950s, and this indeed makes him powerful, just as organising the International Style Show of 1932 or the Deconstruction Show at MoMA, 1988 gave him individual influence and control. However, poignantly, like Prince Charles who also occasionally denies he has any real power, Johnson sometimes says he has very limited power. This is partly true because there are many kinds of power (think of the antinomies – negative and positive, controlling and creative, coercive and persuasive). Having economic, political and coercive power does not lead to creative power. At least among individuals.

View of AT&T, IBM and Trump Towers, taken from Philip Johnson's office in the MoMA Tower by Cesar Pelli

I next asked one of New York's biggest capitalists, the owner of the Conde Nast empire, Si Newhouse, the same question, and he gave an interesting and, I suppose, appropriate answer for a man who owns many of the top magazines, from *The New Yorker*, to *House and Garden* to *Vanity Fair*; 'power is writing about power'. This is unexpected. We usually think power resides in the State, in government, big business and law; that it is either political, or judicial, or economic – the power over people, the power to coerce, to force, to control – not the power to persuade, or use words. 'Power is writing about power' especially today in the major newspapers and key journals. The fourth estate, the media in an electronic world, can make or break empires. From the fall of totalitarian systems in 1989 to the saturation of Diana's marital troubles, we can see the power of the written, recorded and televised word.

Power, it was Michel Foucault's great pleasure to observe, is much more dispersed than we usually think, residing in unlikely places such as languages, sciences – even residing in the human body. There is macro-power that we always name, the State and large corporations and the many micro-powers that we usually fail to observe; the daily exercise of choice, the semi-autonomy of the producer and consumer, choosing their products, friends and lifestyle. If power is everywhere and in everything, then knowing this truth increases, by itself, the amount of dispersed power. People are often enslaved by mental constructs which they never question, and the minute they challenge the convention, or taboo, it can dissolve. So a liberating act is merely the statement that 'power is dispersed, is everywhere, and often up for grabs'. Most people never know it is lying dormant, waiting to be activated.

However, Foucault took a more Darwinian line on this, and said that networks of power are always challenging each other, that the natural state of the human condition is eternal battle' and, reversing Clausewitz, that 'politics is the continuation of war by other means', or 'power [is] a sort of generalised war which assumes at particular moments the forms of peace and the State'. Thus Foucault too slips into aphorism when dealing with the big question.

Hannah Axendt often stressed the way dictatorial power could suddenly vanish, the way Caesar's power could disappear when his followers sensed weakness. This is true, as she pointed out, of totalitarian power and even more true of totalitarian coercion in the electronic village, as we saw again and again in 1989. Coercive power, negative power, vanishes the moment that fear departs.

First, in June the Polish people tested the Brezhnev Doctrine, the party line that force would be used if a country in Eastern Europe left the Soviet sphere of influence – their vote was a partial test; then Hungary tested it slightly more by opening its border to East Germans leaving their country; then the Berlin Wall came down, then Czechoslovakia had its Velvet Revolution, then Bulgaria – in five months five countries left a system when they realised they had nothing to fear. Fear is what I am terming 'negative power', in fact the strongest form of control.

The fastest switch of power structures was in Romania in December, when the dictator Ceausescu appeared in public and suddenly the people, gathered in the main square, realised that, collectively, they had nothing to fear. Power dissolved in five minutes, as soon as they expressed the fact, and no one was quicker to understand this than Ceausescu himself. He fled immediately. If negative coercive power is to remain potent then it must be continuously applied at every moment. This truth Stalin understood and the Chinese understand today: totalitarianism can never relax and it must spread fear throughout every level of society – right up to the top and through the ruling party and ruling families – or else the whole system collapses.

We also know the paradoxes that result from dictatorships: their power can be very fragile, unstable and in that sense weak and likely to vanish if there is an internal power struggle. The potentate can suddenly become, like Ceausescu, impotent. A related paradox is that such totalitarian systems, over time, become weaker than democracies, because they cannot renew what I would call 'positive' or creative power. This depends, and must depend, on the free flow of information. The Soviet Union faced this paradox after 1979 when it became clear that, because of technical innovations, the West's military power had grown way beyond their capacity. The Cold War was won on the electronic battlefields when the 'smart' weapons of the Americans far out performed the 'dumb' armaments pitted against them. Of course these battles took place behind the scenes in client countries, or in Iran and Iraq, but there was no doubt among the Russian ruling class that the West was far stronger and would only become more so, because of their more open system, their constant exchange of information. Perhaps the *Nomenklatura* lost the will to rule, coercively, because they saw that dictatorship was, ultimately, impotent.

This gets at the heart of power which is never as simple as it appears. Indeed the same paradox is evident in the West, and has been since the Vietnam War in the 1960s. Since fighting those tragic and partly absurd battles

AT&T Tower, Philip Johnson, New York

American presidents have come to understand that the Superpower itself can be impotent. It is true America can invade Granada and Panama, and force its will on a tiny country, but in ways that are immoral, that divide its own citizenry. If American power now consists in advanced missiles and nuclear weapons that can never be used, and if it has sold the country to the Japanese to create the fire power – creating nothing but the world's biggest debt – then we have reached the supreme paradox: coercive power not only corrupts, but is suicidal.

There is yet another paradox which our strange times have revealed: power which has no moral direction, or large purpose, also tends to disappear. Most statesmen and elected politicians do not know what to do with the vast forces at their disposal; as was said of President Bush, they lack the 'vision-thing', and without a vision one might as well give it all away. The one time Bush knew what to do – when Saddam Hussein invaded Kuwait – he organised 34 nations into his 'new world order' and created a momentary power structure, thanks to the United Nations and its moral sanction. However, this, the largest collective power in history, lasted for only six months and as long as the purpose was clear-cut. Since then, Bush returned to his usual confused ambivalence, unable to grasp any large situation, whether it is domestic politics in Los Angeles, global warming in Rio, the Kurdish problem in Iraq, or even the presidential election in the USA. Coercive power needs clear, simple and moral direction or else it dissolves. Most people give up power because they do not know what to do with it and unused power does not exist. Or rather, what is power if it leads nowhere and everywhere at once?

It is wrong, or at least incorrect, to speak of power as I am doing in the abstract, as a series of aphorisms that might apply everywhere. In so-called primitive societies a completely different set of relationships exists from those in the West, and in Eastern countries, recently freed from the yoke of totalitarianism, yet another set of conditions prevails. Power is always relative to specific cultural and historical situations. It will be articulated differently in Eastern Germany, which has been under authoritarian dominance for 60 years and only experienced a very few, imperfect years of Weimar democracy in the 20s and 30s. What can an outsider say, except warn, and celebrate positive power, creative potency.

Was it Mao who said 'power grows out of the barrel of a gun', or Lech Walesa who said 'power grows out of the monitor of a television tube'? It is interesting that real architectural power has always rested with the most creative designers, in our century. Sant'Elia, Le Corbusier, the early Mies van der Rohe, Frank Lloyd Wright, Peter Eisenman, Daniel Libeskind, Frank Gehry, Arata Isozaki – you have your own list. Creativity, positive power, gets the last laugh on negative power which must, in the long run, pay its respects. In realpolitik times we have seen Russian dictators defer to Pasternak, Sakharov and Solzhenitsyn though none of their lives was ever made easy – because these writers and scientists had a creative integrity which was well-known, and valued.

Positive power is a positive-sum game, unlike the negative brand, which always has one winner and one loser. In a creative work of architecture or art, everyone gains because you cannot 'own' an experience, and a building is not much diminished by use. As I have implied, those who control the purse strings of power, those who have institutional power, often try to manipulate and influence creative power; Philip Johnson is the supreme example. However, he is critic enough to realise that the creative potency of a Gehry or an Eisenman will deeply influence the present and change it, and will outlast all other forms of power. Creativity is the only revenge of the unempowered over the existing power structures. Like virility and other forms of energy it is a potential everyone has, although few people exploit it. It is not diminished by other people's use, in fact creative power tends to be increased by sharing.

Cultural power, if we call it that, has this extraordinary potential for runaway growth in periods and places motivated by creative ideas and a strong tradition. The Renaissance in Florence is the classic example, with its 45,000 citizens producing an enormous outburst of creative potency which still sustains the city. By contrast, there are approximately 90,000 artists at work today in New York City, and none has the power of a Micaelangelo or Leonardo.

The creative revenge on the uncreative can be gauged by an aphorism of John Wynne-Tyson: 'The wrong sort of people are always in power because they would not be in power if they were not the wrong sort of people'. Michelangelo and Leonardo were always trying to turn the tables on popes and kings; they sometimes succeeded. Moral: in the long run negative power defers to positive power.

Hong Kong and Shanghai Banking Corporation Headquarters, Hong Kong, Sir Norman Foster

ERICA WINTERBOURNE

ARCHITECTURE AND THE POLITICS OF CULTURE IN MITTERRAND'S FRANCE

State patronage of architecture during the Presidency of François Mitterrand has been as substantial as it has been controversial. In what follows, I want to examine the role of the state in the recent cultural and architectural life of France. I hope to show that while there may be many inadequacies in this form of architectural patronage – particularly where there may be overdependency on powerful personalities – the benefits are sufficiently substantial for its justification. I want to suggest that large-scale public patronage, particularly where it is tied to wider policies for urban regeneration, culture and economics, contributes to improving living conditions within cities, and generates employment.

Political involvement has had significant consequences for architecture in France since 1981, the year of Mitterrand's election to the Presidency. Architecture has served as a physical and symbolic vehicle for the policy of cultural 'populism' and 'democracy', adopted by the socialist government. This policy is considered and placed in its historical context: it has entailed an extensive building programme of new cultural institutions, not only in Paris but in many cities throughout France. In addition, the government's policy of decentralisation has generated what is seen to be a 'new urbanism', mainly as a result of the redirection of finances and increased powers of municipal bodies in the provinces. The two policies of greater democracy and decentralisation have been largely instrumental in the birth of what has been called the 'New French Architecture'.

The readiness to build prestigious and conspicuous buildings is to a great extent the result of the climate created by Mitterrand through his patronage of the Grands Projets. The Projets have incited both admiration and ridicule. It is significant that critical appraisal is not infrequently tied to political persuasion in France. Architectural taste is not always disinterested, and the practice of architecture is not untouched by the activities of politicians. The qualities which make a building popular – and therefore successful – for those who aim for a greater 'democratisation' of culture, are often the very qualities which for others make a building vulgar. Therefore, political involvement is not always benign. The history of recent French architecture provides salutary reminders of the less positive aspects of political involvement.

In a recent article on the French pavilion, at Seville in 1992 , the critic François Chaslin commented on the problem of buildings and representation, and on the difficulty of national symbolism 'in a time of identity crises'. The subject for representation in question was a very lofty idea – 'the idea of France'.

In the article, Chaslin remarked on the supporting literature provoked by the competition for the pavilion, and on the almost inevitable mixture of aesthetic doctrine and pretentious ideology which it contained. Specifically, France was described in one entry as a 'tree of liberty' (Valode and Pistre), and in another as a nation which 'stirs the world' (Castro). Significantly, the winning entry of Viguier, Jodry and Seigneur made reference to the Presidential Grands Projets of François Mitterrand. Their claim – which Chaslin characterised as displaying 'touching politi   ¬pportunism' – was that by his architectural choices, Mitterrand had opened a 'path of expression' which brought architecture closer to the ideals of the French Revolution. The return to primary forms – the sphere, cube and pyramid – bore witness to the emergence of a 'new model of society' and the 'ideal of a revival of man'.

The above claims are revealing. Whatever the competitive excesses of '*blabla idéologique*', these claims are not explicable simply in terms of nationalistic posturing. In all cases cited by Chaslin, what is significant is the ideological aspect of the pavilion, and the unquestioning assumption that the 'idea' of France could be coherently conveyed in architectural form. The pavilion was to be no mere exercise in the display of a country's technological or architectural competence, its attitude to environmental concerns, or straightforward industrial boastfulness. The pavilion of 1992, no less than each of the Grands Projets, was an exercise in cultural self-assertion.

Ultimately, it was to be the President himself who would make the choice of architectural scheme for the pavilion at Seville. Equally significant was the decision that the pavilion should house a library, since Mitterrand was then also marking his second term of office with the construction of the new Bibliothèque Nationale de France in Paris, the last and the largest of his Grands Projets. Chaslin's personal verdict on the pavilion was that it established a precarious balance between a certain official, and consequently pompous style - too conscious of '*la grandeur de la France*' – and a rigorous asceticism which owed its inspiration to minimalist art. This description is interesting, since much of the contemporary debate on the state of French architecture involves, to one extent or another, the degree to which architects should be uninhibited by outside interference, particularly of a political kind. This reflects a larger debate about the role of the state in the wider cultural life of a nation.

At his first presidential press conference, Mitterrand announced his plans for expanding the Louvre – an audacious aspiration since this one institution embodied powerful national and cultural sentiments in France. Visiting the site of Pei's Pyramid at the Louvre subsequently, the President was reported to have stated that 'at the base of all politics is the politics of culture'. The belief that the state has a fundamental and legitimate role in the perpetuation and preservation of national culture has a long history in France. It is against this background that the Grands Projets and the subsequent rise of what has been called 'the New French Architecture' should be seen.

André Malraux, France's first Minister of State for Cultural Affairs (1958-69), passionately felt that a shared common culture was a force for national unity. He commenced a programme of building cultural centres throughout France – the Maison de la Culture – in the belief that greater access would help to eliminate long-standing elitism in the arts and bring about the 'democratisation of culture'. Only 14 such centres were built, but that culture could be institutionalised at all, with a determined egalitarian aim, became an accepted notion in French intellectual life. This partly explains the subsequent presidential fondness for marking a period at the Elysée Palace with a significant cultural building – the most obvious example being the Centre National d'Art et de Culture Georges Pompidou. Pompidou established a precedent for direct involvement in design decisions. Presidential favour has since invariably been placed with the Ministry of Culture, in opposition to the pairing of the Prime Minister with the Ministry of Finance. The alliance of Mitterrand and Jacques Lang between 1981 and 1986 was to be a significant one.

The idea that culture should lose its exclusive, elitist status and become more 'democratic', was to be taken up and politicised in the 60s by socialist theorists and supporters. The left grew increasingly critical, both of the ministry – because of what it saw as an unhealthy dominance over the arts through heavily bureaucratic patronage – and of Malraux himself, because of his Gaullist preoccupation with national unity. They believed that the ministry should play a more active role in a progressive egalitarian transformation of society. In a doctoral dissertation reflecting the militancy of 1968, Jacques Lang wrote: 'Culture is more a result than an ingredient. A soft and docile culture corresponds to an aged society; a combative and independent culture belongs to a living one'. While in opposition in the late seventies Lang stated that 'all cultural action must be against power'.

Mitterrand was elected president in May 1981. He immediately cancelled the eighth five-year plan of the previous government and drew up a two-year Interim Plan of his own. Significantly, it placed cultural and sociocultural factors of development alongside other political priorities of employment, production and national solidarity. Culture was in fact seen to be a source of progressive economic and social development and not something separate and alien to it. Creativity was seen as something which needed freedom from state interference and commercial pressure, but which nonetheless deserved public finance because of its economic potential.

The Interim Plan stated that 'Without claiming the right to impose standards of taste, quality or talent, the State shall contribute to promoting the expression of the highest values, and to preserving the living wealth of cultural, social, regional and ethnic diversity'. Elitism would be combated by greatly extending access to culture, and by correcting imbalances in funding which had traditionally favoured Paris. Decentralisation was to be a major policy for the government as a whole, as was the protection of French culture against what was increasingly seen as an invasion of English-language culture through television, film and publishing. As well as these policies the ministry increased the budget for spending on culture annually until 1985, reversing the contraction which had taken place in the 70s.

It was within this ideological climate that the Grands Projets were conceived. Mitterrand's was a party newly elected to power with a mission to democratise and socialise France and affirm her place internationally. The communiqué from the Elysée Palace for the launching of the competition for la Tête Défense in 1982, gave some indication of what was to come. The library and communication centre which it was to contain, would broadcast 'throughout the universe the messages our country bears'. President Mitterrand intended to re-establish Paris as a cultural centre of world status through a programme of civic state patronage. The programme was to be both catholic and progressive, and architecture was to be the conspicuous and symbolic vehicle. It was also a programme which was to give momentum to similar civic-minded regenerations throughout France under the policy of decentralisation.

Mitterrand acknowledges past errors in Utopian thinking about the city 'which rationalises to excess', and the 'inhumanity of imperious efforts which . . . neglect or crush the multiplicity of significations, paths, symbols which make city life lively and livable'. Instead, the 'new instruments of culture' are seen by Mitterrand to rally behind a certain idea of the city – of a collective lifestyle. It also seems clear that compared to previous leaders of France whose aspirations were decidedly imperialist and Roman, his inspiration was far more high-minded and Hellenic.

It was fortunate for Mitterrand that he had a charismatic and popular Culture Minister supporting his efforts. On coming to office in 1981, Lang announced 'I want the ministry to expand, to abuse its own prestige. It should contaminate the state, and the entire nation'. In addition to the wholehearted support of the ministry, Mitterrand could count to a large extent on the support of the Mayor of Paris, Jacques Chirac (1977-86), who was to become his Prime Minister in opposition in 1986. He took the pragmatic view that Mitterrand's projects would help to *revaloriser* the city and complement his already established plans for the *réaménagement* of large areas of Paris. Chirac's support also explains why the building policy was continued after the right returned to power in 1986, despite some opposition from within his own party. Paris was regarded as more important than party political divisions.

The President therefore met with very little obstruction in the early stages of his programme. The Grands Projets were seen in both respects as capital gains. A major cultural building, such as a new museum, would be a driving force for the revitalisation of a district hit by industrial decline and poor infrastructure. A number of schemes for the *réaménagement* of Paris, initiated through the Zone d'Aménagement Concertée classification (ZAC), have benefited in this way. As recently as 1991 competitions were held to begin the redevelopment of the ZAC Seine-Rive-Gauche, the centrepiece of which is the Bibliothèque Nationale. This is the largest urban regeneration scheme in Paris, covering an area of 130 hectares with a planned 2,000,000m^2 of building. The city is financing 320 housing projects this year, and 700 are planned for the next two years on either side of the BNF. Because of the strategic importance of the library to the city, a new metro line is being built and connections with the TGV are being improved. A new pedestrian footbridge is planned to cross the Seine to connect with the park at Bercy. Paris is being 'rebuilt to accommodate the library'.

Criticisms are legion. The library is expected to be functionally inadequate and overdependent on technological solutions. Perrault's defence of his scheme however, is almost entirely in terms of the library's role and relationship to the city, and conforms to Mitterrand's sympathies for greater urban equality and democracy. Formally, the theme is continued by what Perrault describes as the 'democratic' nature of his building. To create a welcoming place he has deliberately avoided imposing entrances and monumental walls, and he talks of reducing the presence of the building in the city through *'l'absence'* of the facades. The esplanade, the four hectares of transplanted Fontainebleau Forest and the important new connections established with the river and with Bercy, are each part of a greater urban strategy. 'Empty' spaces are seen by Perrault as a necessary luxury of city life, fundamental to the democratic nature of city living. In addition, the *bibliothèque* is located in the east of Paris in a deliberate attempt to redress the problem of *déséquilibre* between the west and east of Paris. The *bibliothèque* is a *grande geste* therefore, not to be judged solely on functional performance. It is also the last, and certainly the largest, of Mitterrand's monumental 'gifts' to the Nation.

The Grands Projets do not permit stylistic generalisations. He has declared a taste for simple, geometrical forms, but there is an eclecticism in Parisian architecture which, it might be argued, is also aesthetically democratic. Other than their monumentality and their scenographic locations, there are no simple distinguishing features of the Grands Projets. They are undoubtedly 'symbolic' – L'Arche being the most totemic in this respect, sitting as it does at the head of 'one of the most culturally loaded axes in the world'. It is perhaps understandable that Jacques Lang declared that 'only a grand gesture could measure up to La Défense' where 'measure might mean excess'.

Placing new building at the forefront of regeneration schemes has not been confined to the capital. As a consequence of the government's policy of decentralisation, municipal councils were given autonomy from Paris in March 1982, ending a period of centralised administration which had existed for 200 years. The positive building climate of the capital inspired urban renewal schemes in many cities, frequently with the financial support of the Ministère de l'Equipement, du Logement, des Transports et de la Mer.

One of the features frequently admired by architects in Britain is the power of mayors across Europe to initiate projects, and the regular if not mandatory use of open competitions for public building schemes. Foster's art gallery for the city of Nîmes was the result of an international competition arranged by Jean Bousquet, the newly elected mayor intent upon marking his *emprise* after 30 years of communist municipal government. The tradition of using competitions for public works has been a means of avoiding *copinage* and unhealthy liaisons of interests. As Claude Parent explains, juries have had a moral, democratic function usually guaranteed by the quality of jurors – chosen by ministerial decree. Any underlying pressures from 'the corridors of power' would be to some extent dissipated and would remain hidden. Any error of judgement would rest with the jury and, significantly, not with the state or commissioning authority. Competitions have also helped young architects to gain important commissions, since often the competition entries are anonymous. The quality of a scheme alone is expected to determine choice. Juries thus became recognised democratic arbitrators whose judgements were respected, even at presidential level. The use of international juries has also been seen to raise the quality of architecture throughout France, by avoiding the 'mediocrity of national clan squabbles'.

This policy of decentralisation has engendered a revival of civic patriotism and competitiveness which has been compared to the princely rivalries of Renaissance cities. The newly conferred powers under the policy of decentralisation, has led to what Chaslin describes as a 'psychological war of position' in the provinces. In a time of rapidly rising unemployment municipal authorities of cities such as Nîmes, Lyons and Montpellier have orchestrated competitions and programmes of building to attract industry, commerce and tourism to their cities. These schemes were often initiated by forward looking and newly powerful mayors, intent on raising the profile of their city in advance of the greater European Market of 1992. The 'new urbanism' which has resulted has used architecture to display the vigour and vitality of a city.

It can therefore be said that it is largely politics which has generated the 'New French Architecture'. In a period when a number of governments elsewhere embarked on the systematic withdrawal from large-scale state provision in public life, and the gradual transfer of responsibility for national infrastructure to the private sector, France embarked on a huge building programme financed largely by the public purse. It is estimated that 3,000,000

people should benefit from the 546 planned interventions for the transformation of *les grands ensembles*. The active building programme has generated employment, and is being seen to begin the gradual but co-ordinated improvement of living conditions.

However, this is not the whole story. The Socialist policy of support for cultural activities was argued partly on the basis that it would ultimately contribute to the national economy. During the government of 1981-1986 the costs of maintaining this cultural policy rose significantly, in no small part because of the costs of the Grands Projets. The proportion of the culture budget which they consumed rose from 15% to 70% and the total cost to France by 1987 was 15.5 billion francs in a time of economic recession.

Mitterrand played a crucial role in maintaining the financial commitment to the Grands Projets. They were, after all, a presidential rather than a governmental programme. Not only were building costs significant, but predictions for running costs of the new cultural centres had been over-optimistic. In terms of the benefits to Paris, there has been criticism that tourists have been the major beneficiaries of the schemes, and that the regeneration driven by the Grands Projets has had the effect of gentrifying a number of neighbourhoods at the expense of resident populations, particularly around the Bastille district and at La Villette.

However, decentralisation which permitted aspiring mayors to enhance their territory, has also allowed party politics to dominate cultural affairs. In some areas, cultural policy itself became a political issue to the extent that, by 1986, it was a significant subject for debate at the municipal elections. The Grands Projets were seen by many on the right as expensive excesses of socialist arrogance. More significantly there were increasing concerns over the growth of ministerial power and *dirigisme* which reflected presidential humour and proximity to elections, rather than need. In the year prior to the municipal elections of 1986 funding for cultural projects to the regions, granted through the policy of decentralisation, fell by 50% (126 to 63,000,000 francs), principally to speed the construction of the Grands Projets in Paris. This obviously caused resentment, and ultimately compromised the policy of decentralisation.

The personal instigation and close supervision of the Grands Projets by Mitterrand during the 80s, has led to accusations that he has built by imperial *fiat*. He personally selected Pei as architect for the Grand Louvre, since he regarded the Louvre as too important an institution to be subject to the vagaries of a competition. The Bastille Opera was awarded on the basis of a short list drawn up for the

La Pyramide du Louvre, I M Pei, Grand Louvre, Paris, 1983

president, not by competition, and Nouvel's Institute du Monde Arabe was the result of a competition, but only after Mitterrand had decided unilaterally to cancel an earlier project and launch his own. He also abandoned the schemes developed for the Tête Défense and ran a new competition. Perrault's commission for the Bibliothèque Nationale was ultimately the choice of Mitterrand after a jury had presented him with a short list.

There have been many criticisms that architecture is exploited for political 'game playing'. In an article reminding architects of the dangers of leaders associating themselves with national destiny, Parent talks of the complicity of architecture when used as an affirmation of power. The Bastille, steeped as it is with liberal left-wing associations, was not a politically neutral site for the new 'democratic' opera-house. Mitterrand also timed announcements and exploited ceremony to coincide with political campaigns. Two months prior to the presidential elections of 1988, he conferred the Légion d'Honneur on Pei at a ceremony inside the incomplete Pyramid, and chose Bastille day of the same year to announce his plans for the Bibliothèque Nationale.

The Grands Projets gradually became a major focus for political expression in a new *Querelle* between the progressive left and the more conservative right. In an article titled *'Grands Louvre, Prisme Changeant de l'Opinion'*, Chaslin reveals the extent of changes in opinion in the national press concerning the Louvre Pyramid, which became a barometer of political sympathies. In advance of the municipal elections of 1986, and the presidential elections of 1988, the national press clearly aligned itself either for, or against, the Pyramid. Predictably, *Le Figaro* and *Le Monde*, all sympathetic to the right, denounced the Pyramid wholeheartedly. Mitterrand was accused of *pharaonism*, and labelled 'Mitterramses I', whilst the building was described as vulgar 'vanity jewellery', but as Chaslin notes – these things have nothing to do with taste.

There have been many other criticisms of the Grands Projets, which contain some allegations of political involvement in architecture. Architects are increasingly claiming a loss of independence and liberty, in the face of what Parent describes as the slow and sure degradation which follows a winning competition. A recent and vociferous debate occurred over the Bibliothèque Nationale. In October, 1991, an open letter was published, signed by 566 researchers and academics, complaining of the impracticalities of the future library. The letter stirred a passionate defence from the profession. A petition published in *L'Architecture d'Aujourd'hui,* signed by 400 French

architects, portrays architecture as the innocent target in what was actually a political debate.

The circumstances surrounding the commissioning and awarding of building projects has also been called into question. The democratic and accountable nature of architectural competitions has recently revealed its fragility. Decisions are increasingly overridden or reversed . In such circumstances, juries become merely consultative. In 1988, the redundant grounds of the Ministère de l'Equipement, the most expensive land in Paris, became available for development after their installation in L'Arche. A competition was arranged for the development of the site by architects backed by independent construction companies, to be run concurrently with the receipt of bids from development companies for the land. The highest bid would then be combined with the best scheme and the two bodies would align their costs.

Despite control of the competition by the Mission Interministérielle pour la Qualité des Constructions Publiques, the Ministry of Finance secretly established a level below which offers would be refused. Only one bid for the land was received above this limit, but was disregarded when, by ministerial manoeuvre, it was matched by a preferred developer. In addition, the winning competition scheme by Parent, was *déjugé* by another minister, in favour of the scheme backed by the very construction company who had raised its bid to match the highest offer. In both cases ministerial intervention went against what was supposed to be an ethical operation for ensuring the choice of the most popular scheme. After three separate court cases – one brought by the architect who lost the commission, the second by the developer who had his offer matched, and the third by a local residents' association complaining contraventions of planning regulations – all three judicial decisions found the state acting illegally.

The system therefore has its failings. Powerful individuals are prepared to ride roughshod over procedures, and local objections, in a less than democratic manner. These manipulations of architectural choice are seen by some to favour an official 'state culture' which is no longer clearly disinterested, and which does not feel the need to justify its choices or legitimise criteria.

Not disconnected with the above state of affairs is the influence which elections can have on the quality of design. Proximity to an election can effect the speed with which a building project is conceived, announced and awarded. The importance of the initial presentation results, it is argued, in formalist schemes easily digestible without much analysis. Furthermore, in order to reduce the mounting costs

Parc de la Villette, Bernard Tschumi, Paris, 1982-83

associated with holding competitions, time limits for submission are shortened. This can affect the degree to which detailed attention is given to a scheme, and leads to lengthy and expensive reworking at a later stage.

The petition signed by French architects following the debate on the Bibliothèque Nationale reveals many of the above frustrations, although it also, paradoxically, reveals a confidence in what is seen to be the revival of architecture in France. Architects are now calling for an appropriate recognition of their professional skills, and for the sort of freedom from interference which is ordinarily regarded to be the privilege of artists alone.

At the beginning of the 80s, French architecture was generally felt to be in a moribund state However, journals which at the beginning of the 80s regularly presented foreign buildings were by the close of the decade concentrating on the many new French buildings under construction. There is now generally a recognition of the improvements in quality and inventiveness of French architecture. It could be argued that this success is a direct consequence of the cultural policy, and the policy of decentralisation, initiated by Mitterrand. The Grands Projets have provided *une bouffée d'oxygène* to French architecture. They have not been built in isolation, nor entirely at the expense of public provision of housing, hospitals, libraries and schools. Museums have been an antidote to *dépeuplement* and have helped the *reconquette* of public space – the site of IMA and the Cour Napoléon were notoriously unwelcoming places, particularly at night. Though not perfect, there has been a concerted effort to balance development in Paris between the needs of business and the needs of inhabitants by preventing an over provision of commercially funded office space at the expense of affordable public housing.

A telling contrast now exists in attitudes to the commissioning of public buildings between France and Britain. According to a recent Arts Council publication, 'Architecture and Executive Agencies', public officials in Britain do not generally regard commissioning architecture as a good thing. Indeed, it is considered a 'career risk', especially conspicuous architecture; while in France regarded as a civic asset.

Public initiatives for urban renewal are now common throughout France, under the guidance of such bodies as the Delegation Interministérielle a la Ville. The Ministère de l'Equipement actively promotes its work. The revitalised construction industry is not confined only to public building programmes however, nor is it confined to major cities. As small and isolated a town as Laguiole in the Aveyron, boasts a dramatic steel-clad factory by Philippe

Starck. Internationally, France is now confidently 'exporting' culture, as the now completed French Institute in Budapest testifies.

It would perhaps be naive to suppose that a national cultural policy could operate totally free from intrigue, financial controversy or the sort of political manipulation which has been described above. The pressures in Paris for speculation are no less than in London, and French bureaucracy is notoriously cumbersome. The difference between the policies for urban regeneration in Britain and France however, is that in France, in tandem with private schemes, there are important commissioning bodies investing in public building. These bodies have views about the regeneration of cities which can take a broader view of what might count as the positive consequences of investment. They are also, ultimately, publicly answerable for their decisions. As Renard points out – the Grands Projets have a certain 'cultural logic' and a political justification. They help to *valoriser* and *fédérer la ville*. This is in addition to their established popularity. If the current right-wing government in France chooses to place emphasis on renovation and preservation of the heritage, they are nonetheless beneficiaries of the new cultural climate.

The cost of maintaining support for cultural institutions inevitably places a burden on the State, and the government has now a policy of encouraging private sponsorship. In 1987, tax incentives were introduced by the right-wing coalition, to encourage firms and private individuals to sponsor cultural activities. It might be argued that this is a predictable withdrawal. However, both François Léotard and Jacques Toubon have fought for continued commitment to public spending on the arts. Culture is no longer strictly tied to a particular political party or ideology. As Renard argues, the question for governments is not one of resisting the spread of public support for the arts. The question is one of resisting the argument which states that, since there are no specific conditions for promoting artistic production, is it reasonable not to intervene at all.

Despite the brevity of the above article, I have attempted to convey a balanced picture of the public patronage of architecture in France during Mitterrand's Presidency. There are certainly shortcomings with the procedures for commissioning architecture, and there have been circumstances in which architects have felt that their artistic or professional integrity has been compromised. Nonetheless, it seems to me that the situation as it exists in France, is certainly preferable to the situation where, say, the public commissioning of architecture is conducted on the basis of a civil servant's personal career considerations.

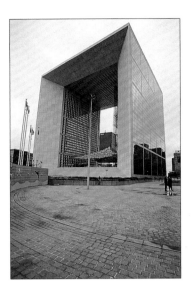

L'Arche de la Défense, Johann Otto von Spreckelsen, Paris, 1989

FRANZ SCHULZE
PHILIP JOHNSON: LIFE AND WORKS

While there has never been a clear consensus about the merit of Philip's architecture overall in the 80s, it seems fair to affirm that he arrived at the end of the decade better known than ever but no closer to the stature of a major master than he had been at the beginning. Too few of the buildings he made garnered the praise sufficient to overcome or compensate for the many that aroused genuine critical hostility. The way had not yet been found by which he might elevate himself above the reach of the perennial judgement 'controversial,' while at the same time he remained both vivacious and combative enough to make the most of it, since it was clearly better than being ignored. Immortality, if it was ever to be conferred upon his architecture, would have to wait.

Meanwhile, he had more to do than design buildings. His approach to the universe of architecture called for action and confrontation at both the public and professional levels, and in those contexts he had lost none of the lustre attributed to him in 1979 by Martin Filler, a critic who could hardly have been called a staunch admirer:

> Philip Johnson has established for himself a unique place in the cultural world of New York (and, consequently, the nation). He is not only trustee, board member, and man about town: he is the Godfather, the Power Broker, the Grey Eminence, the Fount of all Honours for the architectural profession (and, consequently, the nation). Through his support of several institutions and many young architects, his frequent job referrals (Johnson has accepted only a fraction of the architectural commissions offered him, and habitually passes on the rest), and his easy movement between the shapers of ideas and the holders of power, Johnson has consolidated a position unequalled by anyone else in the architecture world today.

No critic anywhere had as uncharitable a view of Philip as Michael Sorkin did, and no architect preyed on Michael Sorkin's mind as did Philip. It was reasonable, then, that Sorkin took the opportunity to record the scenario that led to the 'Deconstructivist Architecture' exhibition of 1988, which Philip curated – for the first time since the early 50s – at The Museum of Modern Art (MoMA). In an article of December 1987 titled 'Canon Fodder' Sorkin reported that a pair of young Chicago architects, Paul Florian and Stephen Wierzbowski, had conceived an idea as early as 1984 for an exhibition of recent architecture marked, in Sorkin's words, 'by a prevalent tendency, shared with the culture in general.' It was 'an architecture obsessed with fragmentation and instability, "torn between history and technology."'

Having assembled a list of 40 to 50 suggested examples, Florian and Wierzbowski applied to the National Endowment for the Arts for grant assistance. They were turned down twice. They then reduced the size of their show and added a title: 'Violated Perfection: the Meaning of the Architectural Fragment.' Another application was prepared and rejected.

Enter Aaron Betsky, employed at the time as an architect in Frank Gehry's Los Angeles office. Lunching one day with Wierzbowski, Betsky was much taken with what he heard about the show and said he would try to find a place for it on the West Coast. Later, he changed his mind, deciding the whole idea was better presented in the form of a book, which he proceeded to peddle to a New York publisher. Florian and Wierzbowski would collaborate.

Sorkin continued, 'However, the same day that Betsky cut his deal at Rizzoli, he had lunch with Philip Johnson.'

Now Sorkin thickened the plot, noting that all this was happening against the backdrop of a search for someone to fill a greatly coveted position at The Museum of Modern Art, the directorship of the Department of Architecture and Design, open since the recent death of Arthur Drexler and tended on acting basis by the Curator of Design, Stuart Wrede. Johnson had taken it upon himself to conduct a search for Drexler's successor, subjecting a number of bright young men to scrutiny over lunch at the Four Seasons. One of these was Betsky, another Joseph Giovannini, a writer for *the Times*, who was himself at work on a book dealing with a subject roughly like that pursued by Betsky. Both Betsky and Giovannini informed Johnson of their respective studies, and Johnson, conversing with Betsky, said he thought 'Violated Perfection' would make a splendid exhibition at MoMA.

Ludwig Mies van der Rohe and Philip Johnson in front of the Seagram Building, New York, 1959

Meanwhile, Wrede, who had hopes of securing the Architecture and Design job for himself but who was 'widely considered', in Sorkin's words, 'to be without Johnson's support,' entertained a phone call from Philip, which included a proposal that the exhibition be put on at the museum. Sorkin wrote:

> Poor Wrede. If ever a man were trapped between a rock and a hard place, it was he. Here's the guy who holds The key to his future, 'all enthusiastic' to do a show as soon as possible, demanding a favour . . . Finally, though, this is the portrait of a man with only one choice, and he made it: the show's being hustled into a slot in June, absolute record time as these things go . . .

Part of the reason for such alacrity was that Wrede, on his own and more independently than Sorkin implied, was strongly in favour of the show and wanted to press forward with it. Even so, this had little effect on Philip's personal momentum. Sorkin went on:

> Now, of course, Philip was obliged to perform power-brokering's primary act: deciding who's in and who's out . . . The initial cut had been done by Florian, Wierzbowski, Giovannini, Betsky, et al, but things needed to be finalised, and so the scene was set for a ritual of consensus and compliance, a transfer of rights from the originators to the appropriator. And, as with so many of the ceremonies of the Johnson cult, this one was enacted at a boys-only dinner at – where else? – the Century Club.
> On October 28, the following gathered in a private room: Philip, John Burgee, Peter Eisenman, Frank Gehry, Aaron Betsky, Joe Giovannini, and Peter Zweig and Mark Wigley, two young academics recently elevated to the Johnson retinue . . . Not present were Florian and Wierzbowski, completely cut out, never having received, as Wierzbowski recently wrote me, a single 'letter or phone call regarding "Violated Perfection", our opinions about it, or a request for permission to use the title.'

Philip's reply to the charges against him was, as Martin Filler reported, 'that the idea was as much "in the air" as the architecture itself.' In his catalogue preface, he did acknowledge Florian and Wierzbowski for inventing the name 'Violated Perfection,' even though the museum, found it unpalatably suggestive, and disallowed it in favour of 'Deconstructivist Architecture.'

Nonetheless, by the time the show was ready for mounting, Philip's manoeuvring had already done damage to his own position and was about to do more; seldom, in fact, has an exhibition been so scalded before it went on view as was this one. After charging him with 'an abuse of power [and] intellectual shoddi-

ness ' Herbert Muschamp, writing two months before the opening, added:

> I hope it is a great show. But I'm not so sure – it seems to me a strong possibility that Philip Johnson resembles the persona Walter Pater fashioned for the *Mona Lisa*, a figure 'older than the rocks among which she sits; like the vampire, she has been dead many times, and learned the secrets of the grave'.

That was a rhetorical back-of-the-hand, of course, but the whole exhibition was overgrown with rhetoric, the densest of it appearing in the literature written to rationalise the work of the architects represented. There were eight exhibitors, all with internationally respected credentials: Frank Gehry (based in Los Angeles), Bernard Tschumi and Peter Eisenman (New York), Zaha Hadid (London), Rem Koolhaas (Rotterdam), Daniel Libeskind (Milan), and Wolfgang Prix and Helmut Swiczinsky of the firm Coop Himmelblau (Vienna). While each of them was distinguishable from the others, their work as a whole tended toward several discernible expressive characteristics: the use of warped and disengaged planes, deviations from parallels and right angles, and, in Philip's own words in the catalogue preface, 'the diagonal overlapping of rectangular or trapezoidal bars.' The emphasis in most of the projects was aggressively formalist, as if little concern had been felt by the designers, let alone shown, for the goals of convention as communication that much of post-modernist architecture had set for itself.

If the exhibition could have been presented independently of all the talk about Philip's motives and all the sweaty theoretical struggles over the concept of deconstructivism, it might have made a more affirmative impression on the critics. But motives and theory were so much at the heart of it that public attention to the work itself was greatly diverted to the margins of consciousness. The irony was that Philip, who had always depended on his eye rather than on theory in judging architecture, had now invited Mark Wigley to write the main catalogue essay, which turned out to be a litany of theoretical maunderings that generated more critical heat than the work it was meant to be about. Wigley began with several massive generalisations as debatable as they were encompassing and undocumented:

> Architecture has always been a central cultural institution valued above all for its provision of stability and order. These qualities are seen to arise from the geometric purity of its formal composition.
> The architect has always dreamed of pure form, of producing objects from which all instability and disorder have been excluded.

He then sought to establish a link between

Philip Johnson in his New York office, 1950

deconstructivism and the efforts of the early Russian constructivists, whose:

> 'impure', skewed, geometric compositions [stood for] a critical turning point where the architectural tradition was bent so radically that a fissure opened up through which certain disturbing architectural possibilities first became visible. Traditional thinking about the nature of the architectural object was placed in doubt. But the radical possibility was not then taken up. The wound in the tradition soon closed, leaving but a faint scar. These [deconstructivist] projects reopen the wound . . .
> If [they] in a sense complete the enterprise, in so doing they also transform it: they twist constructivism. This twist is the 'de' of 'deconstructivist.' . . . The forms themselves are infiltrated with the characteristic skewed geometry, and distorted. In this way, the traditional condition of the architectural object is radically disturbed . . . The internal disturbance has actually been incorporated into the internal structure, the construction. It is as if some kind of parasite has infected the form and distorted it from the inside. The rooftop remodelling project in this exhibition, for example [by Coop Himmelblau], is clearly a form that has been distorted by some alien organism, a writhing, disruptive animal breaking through the corner. Some twisted counter-relief infects the orthogonal box. It is a skeletal monster which breaks up the elements of the form as it struggles out . . .
> The more carefully we look, the more unclear it becomes where the perfect form ends and its imperfection begins: they are found to be inseparably entangled . . . It is as if perfection had always harboured imperfection, that it always had certain undiagnosed congenital flaws which are only now becoming visible. Perfection is secretly monstrous.
> Tortured from within, the seemingly perfect form confesses its crime, its imperfection.

Wigley's explicit denial that the work on view was an application of the literary theory of deconstruction hardly cleared things up, especially in view of the claim lodged about the same time by Giovannini:

> And just as a literary text, according to advocates of deconstruction such as Jacques Derrida and the late Paul de Man, doesn't have a unifying wholeness or fixed meaning, but several asymmetrical and irreconcilable ones, a building can consist of disparate 'texts' and parts that remain distinct and unaligned, without achieving a sense of unity.

Indeed, Wigley's constant references to parasites and other alien organisms and invasive monsters bore a suspiciously strong resemblance to the usages of Derrida, but no less to the favourite phraseologies of Eisenman, whom Wigley knew through common connections at Princeton University. Eisenman, who was promoting Derrida heavily at the time, while seeing a lot of Philip, loved to apply words like *contamination* and *transgression* to architecture, sprinkling them throughout the conversations he had with Philip as early as their failed series of biographical interviews in 1982. The press was collectively unsympathetic toward the exhibition, scoring it over and over, as Brendan Gill wrote, with 'reviews so harsh that even the Broadway euphemism "mixed reviews" . . . would amount to an overly benign summary of them.' Douglas Davis attacked as 'preposterous' Wigley's assertion that the deconstructivist architects were 'shocking', adding that 'it overlooks the virulent, mocking, anti-art tradition that has coursed through the entire century.' Herbert Muschamp was heard from again, in no happier a mood following the show than prior to it:

> Nor do the ideas with which Wigley promotes the doctrine of impure form arise from the centre of architectural practice (or, for that matter, from Russia during the teens). They have drifted into his impressionable mind from post-structural philosophy as it developed in Paris following the student uprisings of 1968: buzz words like strategy, agent, intervention, subversion, undermine, disrupt, extremity, enigma; prêt-à-penser modes like the ecstasy over instability and the collapse of meaning . . .

Thus Wigley caught more of the critics' displeasure than did the architects, whose work on the whole was greeted with polite praise ('I don't see much theoretical intensity in Zaha Hadid's work, but her visual intelligence is acute,' said Muschamp) or something close to a shrug ('There is nothing abrasive or startling in these buildings,' wrote Jane Holtz Kay). Philip himself was seen, by consensus, as the string pulling mastermind of the event. Some observers, unwilling to accept his claim that deconstructivists was not a style, movement or creed but just a 'confluence of a few important architects' work of the years since 1980,' insisted he was trying to do again what he had done in the MoMA 'Modern Architecture' show of 1932; namely, illuminate the most promising pathway that a vital new architecture might follow – specifically, in this case, away from an ageing post-modernism to something called deconstructivism. Probably the critics were right, and it was unlikely that they would have resented him for such a motive, taken by itself. What most aggrieved them was their impression that he had achieved his ends through an imposition of naked power: 'the use of MoMA as a platform for old boy promotion,' as Douglas Davis declared just before enunciating his central complaint: 'that the exhibition had little to do with the art of architecture and everything to do with polemics.'

Philip was trapped in an irony. His practised eye – no one contended it was less than that – was evident in the overall merit of the eight architects he chose, but it was compromised by his willingness to avert it, to allow the theoreticians to take command of the temple.

Therewith, another parallel with his experience in the 1932 exhibition comes to mind. He always freely admitted he had profited in that venture from all he learned from two brilliant colleagues, Alfred Barr and Henry Russell Hitchcock. Equally a matter of record is his own observation that he was customarily less comfortable in his professional pursuits when he conducted them all by himself than when he had some such partner at his side. In the case of the deconstructivist show, the voice whispering in his ear, more exactly declaiming, belonged to Peter Eisenman.

There can be no extensive account of Philip's later years without some considerable space allocated to Peter, who was the first to acknowledge his uncommon ability to make space for himself anywhere, any time. Quick-witted, talented, intellectually ambitious, vain, articulate, immensely sociable and capable of the boldest manipulations in the service of professional power, he had manifestly so much in common with Philip, and was in the nature of things so close to him, that the two men seemed virtually destined to an ambivalent relationship that neither could relinquish or fully resolve. Although Peter admitted sharing confidential passages of the 1982 biographical tapes with an outsider, arousing Philip's suspicions, he also claimed that Philip's affection for him derived from his efforts to defend Philip against those who charged him with fascist sympathies. Eisenman was always full of praise for Philip's generosity in helping him recoup business losses by making him a loan of ten thousand dollars – a sum Philip insisted was no loan at all but a kill fee terminating their contract regarding the 1982 biography. Nevertheless, once they reconciled, they stayed that way. In 1990, Philip was best man at Peter's second marriage, to Cynthia Davidson, at Chicago's aristocratic Racquet Club. Peter, in turn delivered an eloquent encomium to Philip at a celebration of the latter's 85th birthday at Seton Hill College, Pennsylvania, in 1991.

If there was one thing they did not share, it was an opinion about psychoanalysis. Philip had done without therapy long enough to dismiss analysis as mostly nonsense. Peter saw

it as the route to ultimate truth. Muschamp once spoke of Eisenman's 'quirky desire to insinuate his private psychoanalytic history into his public persona.' Peter certainly considered himself an expert on the subject even though his perceptibly Jungian opinions were at odds with the more advanced theories of the 90s. On the subject of Philip's politics in the 30s, Peter reflected thus:

He was run by his unconscious, what I would call his anima, which is very active in the homosexual personality. If you've been in psychoanalysis, you realise that part of homosexuality is the female side, the unconscious female side out of control. When Philip runs afoul of everybody, the anima is still the thing that strikes out, and bites, and is nasty. It's this anima that is basically sated through his physical, homosexual, his very satisfactory relationship with David. The anima is fine there. But sometimes it still bites, strikes. If you've been analysed as long as I have . . . I've changed. I've come to understand Philip and to be able to deal with the anima, and so it doesn't threaten me. But I think that Philip went out of control in the 30s.

Needless to say, that statement was not made in the presence of Philip, even though he was not only accustomed to what he regarded as Peter's addiction to high-flown flummery, but most of the time tolerant of it. Frequently, if not typically, he would be offended by something Peter said, then get over it and forgive him. As late as 1988, six years after the payment of the kill fee, Peter, referring to the notorious articles Philip had written in 1939 for Father Coughlin's *Social Justice,* remarked, 'He [Philip] sees nothing wrong with them.'

That was hardly fair of him, Philip rejoined privately, remembering that he had never said anything to Peter on the tapes that warranted such a simplistic summation, especially out of context, but the friendship held fast. Eisenman recalled the Fifth International Exhibition of Architecture of the Venice Biennale in 1991, to which Philip, having been appointed commissioner of the American entry by the exhibition director Francesco Dal Co, chose to show Peter and Frank Gehry. As Peter said:

I can tell you how he chose us. You see, all of these things are so goddamned complicated . . . We got him to be the commissioner so that we could be appointed . . . Frank and I are not naive or blameless. Dal Co came to see me and he said, 'I want you and Frank to come to the United States [slip of the tongue; Peter meant Venice]. How do I work that' . . . I said, 'I can't guarantee you that a committee from the Guggenheim is going to appoint Frank and me . . . The only way I can see it to work it is to get Philip as

ABOVE: The Queen of Thailand, David Rockefeller and Johnson, December, 1991; BELOW, L TO R: Robert AM Stern (New York Architect), Barbaralee Diamonstein (New York author and architectural critic), Johnson and David Whitney (Philip's partner and freelance editor and curator), 1992

the [American] commissioner . . . He's got enough credibility to do it.' . . . And then Philip said to me, 'Well, what should I do? I can either do the young people or do Frank and you.' I said, "Frankly, Philip, you should have me and Frank.' He said, 'Okay!' That's as truthful as I can be about it.'

Peter's willingness to admit wielding influence over Philip's judgement without ensuring that he was talking off the record was a form of daring, a reflection of his conviction that an image of brazenness profited him in the long run. People were certain to talk about him; he would stand out in a crowd. If such an outlook was not a consequence of his own calculation, it had to be something he learned from Philip, who had made great capital of it over the years, frequently and merrily comparing himself with Peck's bad boy. Most important, both men believed that the offence critics took at their behaviour was only rarely of lasting consequence in the world of cultural power.

Yet it is vital to observe that each of them could back up his bravado. Philip's achievements as architect, critic, curator and patron were demonstrably unique in the arts of the twentieth century, while Peter himself had grown by the late 80s into an architect of substance, as his convoluted but inventive – and highly publicised – design for the Wexner Centre at Ohio State University (1990) testified. Moreover, his intelligence, wit and persuasiveness were real. He had as much a right to that place in the Venice Biennale as any of his rivals, and Philip, notwithstanding his wire pulling and dial turning, agreed. Eisenman and Gehry seemed to him at the very top of the middle generation of American architects.

If Peter had much to gain from Philip, he had also much to give. Philip was convinced that Alfred Barr had been a better trained, a more distinguished intellect and a more reliable friend and nobler character. However, Barr was dead now, like Mies and all those others. Thus Eisenman, as well as Stern, Gehry, and the rest of 'the kids,' as it pleased Dean Johnson to call them, were the most engaging people closest to him, each grateful for his interest and more capable than anyone he knew of keeping him where he forever wanted to be, close to the forward edge of the van.

Peter also introduced Philip to a group of young men he had gathered around himself. Wigley was one, another was Jeffrey Kipnis, whose familiarity not only with deconstructionist theory but with Nietzsche and Heraclitus, more Johnson favourites, so engrossed Philip that Kipnis became both his mentor and protégé in the late 80s and early 90s. Thus the close connection with Kipnis and Eisenman seemed the best sign that Philip, and they, had been neither defeated nor derailed by the critics' hammering of the Decon show. In 1990, Philip went so far as to publish, at his own expense, a limited edition of aphorisms by Kipnis, *In the Manor of Nietzsche*, and to contribute the introduction, which began with a confession:

I have heretofore taken a stand against Theory in architecture . . . All the exegeses of various theories seemed to me murky, tiresome, boring and, what is more important, not applicable to the problem in front of us: how to build a building.
Now I am converted. The theoretical framework suggested by Kipnis' aphorisms seems to fit my mental work habits . . . I need some useful paradigm of an architectural "truth." I have to believe. Theory is an actual necessity for design.

In fact, what Kipnis was about was not architectural theory in the standard sense but a kind of deconstructionist-based play with ideas – for example, 'a) The meaning of any work is undecidable. b) In as much as they aspire to the meaningful, conventional ways of working, whether radical or conservative, always seek to repress undecidability.'

Theory or whatever, such a statement was music to Philip's anti-Platonic ears; nor could he resist this one: 'All the letters of architecture, all of its theories, its histories and its criticisms desire to design. Distrust those that protest to the contrary; they protest too strongly.' Obviously, that was not theory at all, but something of a rationalisation of Philip's own career as an architect. However much Philip protested, he never really gave up believing in Mephistopheles' counsel to the student in *Faust, Part I*: 'theory, dear friend, is grey.' Thus he satisfied himself with listening, dutifully enthralled, to Kipnis and Eisenman and Wigley and the rest, and even sitting down with Kipnis in front of eager audiences in the United States and Japan. Kipnis knew his Derrida, which made up for the fact that Philip had read just enough of the Frenchman to be put off by what he found a steady impenetrability – just as he had baulked at Whitehead's metaphysics during his undergraduate years. So he and Jeffrey talked at length, brightly and learnedly.

KIM DOVEY
PLACE / POWER

This essay explores a range of questions about the links between the experience of place and the practices of power in architecture. To what extent is everyday place experience a form of 'false' consciousness? What is the nature of power as it operates on and through the built environment? Who profits from the fragmentation of discourses under post-modernism? How are the forms and practices of architecture structured in sectional interest? What is the role of participation in a restructuring of power relations? In particular I am concerned to refute the perceived opposition between a place-based approach to architecture and the ideological critiques of how place experience is constructed and reproduced.[1]

Place and ideology

The place-oriented approach to architecture is primarily based in a phenomenological view that experience in everyday life is the beginning point for a rigorous understanding of meaning, that one cannot assume a pre-reflective world separate from our experience of it. This involves a reassessment of the concept of 'space' in experimental rather than geometric terms, and a concern for the ontology of 'dwelling'.[2] It is an attempt to construct a theory of architectural meaning from its grounded reception in everyday life. Such a concern leads to a hermeneutics of interpretation since architectural meaning is seldom singular and is highly dependent on human action on, and interaction with, the built environment. While meaning may be found to persist in certain forms, the extent to which social and political process brings meaning to form, indeed even opposing meanings to the same form, has the power to undercut any purely formal analysis of architectural meaning. The interaction of people with the built environment is a primary generator of place experience.[3]

The key problem with such an approach is that the focus on experience can involve a certain blindness to the pronounced effects of social structure and ideology on that experience. In a famous passage Marx argued that 'It is not the consciousness of men that determines their existence, but their social existence that determines their consciousness'.[4] From this view phenomenology is research into a kind of 'false consciousness' and a focus on experience runs the risk that underlying ideological structures will remain buried and hence powerful. Bourdieu argues that the built environment embodies a set of divisions and hierarchies which reproduce the social order unconsciously as part of the taken-for-granted context to everyday life. 'The most successful ideological effects' argues Bourdieu, 'are those that have no words, and ask no more than complicitous silence'.[5] It is the 'silent' discourse of architecture, and the way in which it coerces and seduces our silent complicity, that are the source of its deepest associations with power.

Some dimensions of power/place relations are very briefly outlined as follows:

- Myth/History – Architecture inevitably uses metaphor and constructs mythology through a politics of representation. The historically constructed power relations embodied therein can be made to seem natural or authentic and therefore unquestioned. Architecture is seductive, it constructs desire.
- Colossal/Insignificant – The use of colossal scale, in either mass or volume, can both intimidate and seduce the subject into acceptance of forms of domination. Architecture signifies the force necessary to its production.
- Stability/Change – Architecture offers images of a stable social order which serve to legitimate the status quo. 'Archetypal' forms such as the pyramid, with the power to symbolise order and stability may be colonised in the interest of power.
- Disorientation/Reorientation – Architecture orients and/or disorients its subjects through its spatial structure. Places of consumption often disorient the consumer to establish a reorientation according to instrumental imperatives.
- Surveillance/Privacy – Architecture segments space in a manner that places certain kinds of people and action under the surveillance of a normalising regime while privileging other kinds of people and action as private.
- Segregation/Access – Architecture segregates places by status, gender, race, culture, class and age, creating privileged enclaves of access, amenity, consciousness and community.
- Simulation/Distortion – Architecture is

negotiated between architect, client and community using simulations which can be distorted or represented in a manner that inhibits certain interests while privileging others.

One does not need to be a structural determinist to recognise the profoundly important and subconscious effects of ideology as a 'frame of reference' for everyday life. Ideology underlies place experience and placemaking process at all levels – beliefs about the 'good life', the 'nice house', about property, individualism, gender, race and efficiency. The built environment is a primary medium for the techniques of establishing, legitimising and reproducing ideology at every scale from the house to the city.[6]

Without an understanding of the ideological context, design and research activities that aim to make the experience of place more agreeable, can serve to legitimate and reproduce prevailing structures of power. On the other hand, a problem with this kind of ideological explanation of place experience is that it requires a pre-reflective structure to be asserted, it assumes an elite and superior viewpoint, akin to the fish who claims it alone can 'see' the water. To approach the tasks of environmental change from such a viewpoint is to risk imposing an equally oppressive ideology from above, a risk for which we surely have enough chilling reminders. An irony here is that well-meaning designers, in a zest to create a 'sense of place', can often achieve much the same end.

While 'ideology' has a traditional meaning linked to 'false consciousness' it also has a broader meaning in recent theory as a necessary relationship between consciousness and the structures of the material world.[7] As such, 'ideology' is integrated with the 'web of meaning' we call culture. While ideology limits experience and action, it is also necessary to experience and action. To transcend ideology would be to render the world meaningless. What is needed is a framework which integrates place experience and its ideological critique, and which rejects both social structural determinism and the implication of an autonomous subject.

The expropriation of meaning
The task of integration, however, is complicated by the broad shift from modernism to post-modernism, which embodies both liberating aspects and a new 'depthlessness' of cultural life.[8] It involves a shift from ethics to aesthetics, a triumph of surface over depth that in architecture has detached built form from its social context. At the same time the economic value of aesthetics, of architecture as 'symbolic capital', has increased. Architectural style has

become both a form of currency and a decisive component of political life. This detachment of form from social life has allowed a seemingly radical break with modernism to mask a deeper conservatism, a commodification of meaning under the aesthetic guise of a revival of meaning.

The new politics of the image, the power of the surface to subsume matters of substance, is evident in the gallery architecture which dominates much journal discourse and the design studio. Students do not need to understand the theory to become expert in the politics of the studio where they are inducted into a kind of commodity fetishism, a focus on formal product differentiation and away from the site, programme and social context. While the paper architecture of the journals and studios is often seen by its agents as ideological resistance, the formal fetish coupled with the retreat from programme meshes well with the increasing dominance of the exchange value of places over their use value in everyday life.

While the framed architectural drawing gains value as art, as the 'end' rather than the 'means' of architecture, so architectural meaning becomes a means towards the ends of the market. The qualities of lived experience in the built environment, based in use value, become secondary to the quantities of exchange value. The significance of place in people's lives is often reduced to the signification of meaning through a collage of formal imagery, a 'text' to be decoded or read rather than an integral part of a world in which we dwell and act. The semiotic adage that 'there is nothing outside the text' becomes self-fulfilling.

Through this process lived experience itself becomes subject to commodification and reduced to its image. The intangibility of concepts such as 'sense of place' is exploited to legitimise environmental design projects. without rigorous argument. In this way the concept of 'place' is expropriated into the aesthetic mystique of the architecture profession or the market, protected by its intangibility from rigorous analysis.

The market for new meaning creates an appetite for distinction and therefore for increased turnover in fashion. A voracious meaning market demands of architects both the manipulation of taste and new images to feed it. This is part of a process that Harvey calls creative destruction wherein the built environment is persistently and repeatedly destroyed to allow for its own economic recreation. As Ewen puts it: 'Style is something to be used up, part of its significance is that it will lose significance'.[9] This is a process of place destruction in which the architectural profession is deeply implicated.

FROM ABOVE: Places of Consumption may disorientate the consumer for instrumental imperatives. Melbourne Central Shopping Centre, Kumagai Gumi, 1991; the privileged 'medieval' enclave – Laguna Niguel, California, 1991

Symbolic Resistance

Many architects are unwilling to be the mute agents of such a meaning market. The most tempting path of resistance for them is on the symbolic plane, to exploit the gaps and slippages in the semiotic spectacle, and the persistent demands for new meaning, as opportunities for resistance. Using tactics that have worked to some effect in painting, architectural imagery is used to attack the very ideological context which produces it. Much of what we call deconstructionism in architecture is of this kind, where social and ideological issues are 'referred to' through built (or more often drawn) form.

Theoretical support for this approach comes from Adorno who called for aesthetic tactics of displacement and estrangement, the use of art as a kind of weapon in a 'negative dialectic' against instrumental reason. 'A successful work of art . . . ' he argued, 'is not one which resolves contradictions in a spurious harmony, but one which expresses the idea of harmony negatively by embodying the contradictions, pure and uncompromised, in its innermost structure . . . Art . . . is a force of protest of the humane against the pressure of domineering institutions'.[10]

Most such approaches in architecture interpret the programme as instrumental reason, rationality as a veil for power. Yet the response to the programme and social context is generally in the form of symbolic resistance to it as part of the semiotic display, albeit largely illegible to clients and users. Thus social criticism is subsumed into the production of secretly 'critical' buildings that interfere neither with the accumulation of capital nor with the reproduction of social order.

To the extent that symbolic resistance generates symbolic capital, it ironically serves the subject of its criticism. The problem here is that any formal imagery, to be effective, must be powerful. There seems to me to be no reason why the power residing in any image cannot be diverted, at least temporarily into the service of the status quo. This is true for even the most radically de-centred images of deconstruction. While Tschumi's follies at *Parc de la Villette* may avoid a fixed architectural programme, they serve a larger function in legitimating the (post)modern French state. Shopping malls are emerging in deconstructive style, the 'place' to go to get de-centred.

The retreat from programming is a misguided avoidance of a major dimension of power and ideology in architecture. While architecture will always be primarily about formgiving, the retreat from site and programme renders architecture rootless, with little to give form to, except the supposedly autonomous expression of the individual artist. The

increased autonomy of architectural aesthetics protects the power of the profession, albeit in reduced form. Yet it does longer term damage to a profession which gains its legitimacy through its public service in giving aesthetic expression to the framing and sheltering of everyday life. In sum, the triumph of the image under post-modernism is also an expropriation of meaning from everyday life. The syndrome is that the concern to capture and communicate meaning through built form strips architecture of a primary source of meaning in the dialectics of social life. Architecture is tending to deliver more meanings of less and less significance.

Power in architectural practice

One of the strengths of a place-based approach in architecture is that aesthetics is not detached from social life but treated as an internal part of the everyday lifeworld. Architecture is not 'framed' as an object for contemplation, but is itself seen as a 'frame' for action. Yet, such an approach needs to integrate the critiques of ideology with those of what architecture delivers in terms of everyday place experience. This is close to the aims of Giddens' theory of 'structuration'[11] which focuses on the dialectical relationship between social structure and human agency. Agency, in relation to architecture, may be construed as the human capacity to construct or change a building, their relations with it, or human relations within it. This includes everything from the capacity to hang a picture, renovate or demolish, to the capacity to hire or choose an architect, influence design decisions, or tell an architect 'I can't understand'. Agency is the empowerment rather than oppression, manipulation, coercion and authority. Power is rooted in human agency and is not equivalent to exploitation. Social structure both enables and constrains such agency which in turn produces and reproduces social structure.

While there are some sharp differences from Giddens, Foucault also argues that power is not merely a top down hierarchical force of domination.[12] Foucault's major contribution has been in outlining fundamental changes in the nature of power relations since the late 18th century. Modern power, he argues, is productive and operates through the micro-practices of everyday life, through practice rather than belief. He is interested not so much in a decoding of hidden meaning but in articulating the discursive regimes and practices through which power relations are produced and reproduced. This includes everything from the spatial structure of buildings and cities as disciplinary technology, to the micro-practices of body language and journal publication. Unlike the violence which it largely replaces,

FROM ABOVE: The triumph of the image as symbolic capital – advertising the corporate tower, Melbourne, 1990; Serving the ideological programme while denying the functional programme – Parc de la Villette, Paris, Bernard Tschumi

this modern form of power is continuous, cheap, efficient and difficult to target, and its grip is deeper since it turns its objects into self-enforcers. Modern power constructs 'subjects' with an illusion that they are agents.

It follows that liberation does not necessarily come through the overthrow of power since power operates through a kind of capillary action which is more deeply rooted than belief or ideology. Liberation, for Foucault, is a form of practice, and although he avoided the question of the legitimacy of power relations, his work points to a 'politics of everyday life'. If liberation and domination are forms of practice, they cannot be reduced to their various images. While the example of the panopticon offers an architectural metaphor, it does not operate through symbolism but through disciplinary practice. While it is possible to see formal patterns in the architecture of totalitarianism, the social meaning embedded in form is necessary to the practices of domination. The ideology of Nazism found its legitimation in both the monumental neo-classic and in the 'blood and soil' image of the vernacular. What distinguished Nazism was not only its architecture but its effective use of architecture in the social production of meaning.[13]

What much of this theory indicates is that while the meaning market, fed by formal imagery, drives high-style design, there remain deeper layers to architectural experience and practice that are crying out for change. The everyday lifeworld, constrained as it may be by ideology, is the locus of all forms of agency and practice. There is a case for exploring the manner in which power and human agency are negotiated and reproduced through architectural practice. While deconstruction in architecture is strongly associated with a fetish for form that I have argued is highly conservative, deconstruction as method, the 'unpacking' of the forms, theories and practices of environmental design can be very useful. If we are to take seriously the manner in which social process brings meaning to form then what must be deconstructed and reconstructed is the structure of design practice. The task here is to bring to consciousness the manner in which the definitions of design processes and the roles of the agents within them are structured according to certain interests. These are primarily: the interests of capital in the maximisation of profit; the interests of the state in reproducing social order; the interests of the architect in professional reputation, and the interests of inhabitants in better forms of life.

It is when the form and structure of the built environment comes into question and an architect is hired that many of the interesting questions about the reproduction of social

order are raised. The task is to deconstruct the contexts within which designers practice, the forms of reasoning used and the ways in which design communication may be distorted by political and ideological forces. Whose interests are served by framing a design problem in a certain way, by setting certain time frames, by accepting a 'programme' as given? Who benefits from architectural drawings that are indecipherable to the layperson, from a refusal to show function on a plan or from drawings which give a false image of the future? The work of Habermas on systematically distorted communication is useful for such an analysis.[14]

Such a deconstruction implies a reconstruction and the everyday world of practice is the locus of this reconstruction. The design process represents an opportunity for the reconciliation of form and process, of architecture with social context and for the reassertion of the dominance of use value over exchange value. How sustainable is the role of architects as mute agents, supplying fashions for the meaning market, uncritically reproducing the social order? The architectural profession has long faced the dilemma that while its legitimacy depends on community service, they are beholden to those with land, power and money.[15] Is it as Harvey argues that 'the best of architects is reduced to the status of bee in the hive of capitalist society'?[16] I suggest that there is scope for creative resistance, through the role of architects in the production of 'taste', through the deconstruction of the 'programme' and because of their access to the grass roots production of meaning in the design process.

Much of what I have argued implies a framework of community or participatory design. Yet, it is difficult indeed to say what such a process consists of other than a broad range of forms of empowerment. It may lead to control over the programme or the budget, the right to choose the architect, even the choice of whether or not to participate. While there is a substantial amount of literature on participatory design practice, to define what it consists of in advance is clearly self-contradictory. It is easier, and perhaps more important given the misconceptions, to define what it is not. It does not include the slick manipulations of architectural facilitators producing legitimation for another *fait accompli*. Participatory design does not imply that either the users or designers of buildings necessarily have the answers, the skills or the resources, only that the opportunity for environmental change is also a chance for collective empowerment and social change. Community architecture is not limited to the small-scale, it is both necessary and possible at the urban design scale. A basic right to the exercise of human agency in the

FROM ABOVE: The de-centred shopping centre – Doncaster Shoppingtown, Melbourne, Westfield Corporation, 1992; symbolic resistance – entry to community rooms and housing for North Melbourne Tenants Council, 1987. The entry is a symbolic 'prop' for disempowered clients for whom there is no redemption through architecture (architects, Ashton Raggat)

built environment does not entail an abandonment to mass culture and opinion polls. Nor does it release the designer from the role of form-giver, participatory design requires more imagination, not less. It should encourage difference, not for its own sake, but because the desire for a better (hence different) built environment is the source of all architecture. If the results are judged banal then we must ask both 'whose fault?' and 'whose taste?'. Participatory design requires a high level of aesthetic judgement coupled with a highly critical attitude to the concept of 'taste' and its social role in the production of class distinction.[17] It also entails a high level of simulation skill to ensure that participants understand decisions that are made. Popular nostalgia for regressive imagery should be met on its own terms with the creative imagination of a future wherein the past is neither erased nor re-created. The forms that result from a participatory process may or may not be radically different, but the break with existing power relations ensures a renewed depth of meaning.[18]

However, should we still call this 'community architecture'? Such a label ultimately makes sense only as the 'other' to the formalism and economic rationalism of a profession that has lost its roots in service to the community. Participatory design is nothing more, or less, than the democratisation of the design process and it suffers from the problems of democracies everywhere. It is a messy, fragmented, multiplicitous system that must be judged against its alternatives. It can be misused as a panacea and as a means of legitimisation, but the fact that elections can be rigged and desire can be manipulated is no argument for dictatorship. Participatory design covers a multitude of design practices and it is by no means the only ingredient of good design practice.

Architecture is necessarily a highly political and social art. It is essentially the imagination and production of a (supposedly) better future in social and aesthetic terms, but where is this better future revealed? Is it in the pristine images of the glossy journals, weighed down with esoteric discourse and protected from lay opinion? Is it in the bank balance where the symbolic capital of the latest image has been cashed? The value of architectural practice is revealed in the everyday experience of the places it creates, constrained as they may be by the imperatives of ideology and power.[19]

Notes

1 For a different approach to a similar issue see: K Dovey, 'Dwelling, Archetype and Ideology', *Center 8*, University of Texas, 1993, pp9-21.
2 See, for instance, D Seamon and D Mugeraue (eds) *Dwelling, Place and Environment*, Martinus Nijhoff, The Hague, 1985; C Norberg Schulz, *The Concept of Dwelling*, Rizzoli, New York, 1985; E Relph, *Place and Place-lessness*, Pion, London, 1976; D Seamon (ed), *Dwelling. Seeing and Designing*, SUNY Press, Albany, 1993.
3 The best account of this position is L Lerup, *Building the Unfinished: Architecture and Human Action*, Sage, Beverley Hills, 1977; See also, K Dovey, 'The Creation of a Sense of Place', *Places 1 (2)*, 1984, pp32-40.
4 K Marx, *A Contribution to the Critique of Political Economy*, Lawrence & Wishart, London, 1971, p21.
5 P Bourdieu, *Outline of a Theory of Praxis*, Cambridge University Press, London, 1977, p188.
6 In increasing scale see, K Dovey, 'Model Houses and Housing Ideology in Australia', *Housing Studies 7 (3)*, 1992, pp177-188; T Markus, *Buildings and Power*, Routledge, London, 1993; K Dovey, 'Corporate Towers and Symbolic Capital', *Environment and Planning B 19*, 1992, pp173-188; B Hillier & J Hanson, *The Social Logic of Space*, Cambridge University Press, Cambridge, 1984; M Sorkin (ed), *Variations on a Theme*, Park Wang & Hill, New York, 1992; S Zukin, *Landscapes of Power*, University of California Press, Berkeley, 1991.
7 P Dickens, 'Social Science and Design Theory', *Environment and Planning B 7 (3)*, pp353-360; R Williams, *Problems in Materialism and Culture*, Verso, London, 1980; B Warf, 'Ideology, Everyday Life and Emancipatory Phenomenology', *Antipode 18 (3)*, 1986, pp268-283.
8 D Harvey, *The Condition of Postmodernity*, Blackwell, Oxford, 1989; H Harris and A Lipman, 'A Culture of Despair: Reflections on Post-modern Architecture',

Sociological Review 38, 1986, pp837-854; F Jameson, 'Postmodernism, or the Cultural Logic of Late Capitalism', *New Left Review 146*, 1986, pp53-92. See also P Harries, A Lipman and S Purden, 'The Marketing of Meaning', *Environment and Planning B 9*, 1982, pp457-466; P Knox, 'Symbolism, Styles and Settings', *Architecture and Behaviour 2 (2)*, 1982, pp107-122; P Clarke, 'The Economic Currency of Architectural Aesthetics', M Diani, and C Ingraham (eds), *Restructuring Architectural Theory*, Northwestern University Press, Evanston, 1989, pp48 - 59; S Ewell, *All Consuming Images: The Politics of Style in Contemporary Culture*, Basic Books, New York, 1988.
9 D Harvey, *The Urbanisation of Capital*, Johns Hopkins University Press, Baltimore, 1985; Ewell, *All Consuming Images*, op cit, p52.
10 T Adorno, *Minima Moralia*, New Left Books, New York, 1974, p224; See also, M Horkheimer and T Adorno, *The Dialectic of Enlightenment*, Continuum, New York, 1972; K Frampton, 'The Status of Man and the Status of his Objects', *Architectural Design 52 (7/8)*, 1982, pp6-19
11 A Giddens, *A Contemporary Critique of Historical Materialism - Vol 1 Power, Property and the State*, University of California Press, Berkeley, 1981.
12 M Foucault, *Power/Knowledge*, Pantheon, New York, 1980; M Foucault, 'Space, Power and Knowledge', S During (ed), *The Cultural Studies Reader*, Routledge, London, 1993, pp161-169; N Fraser, *Unruly Practices*, University of Minnesota Press, Minneapolis, 1989.
13 B Lane, *Architecture and Politics in Germany, 1918-1945*, Harvard University Press, Cambridge, 1968; P Dickens, 'The Hut and the Machine', *Architectural Design*, January, 1981, pp18-24.
14 J Mayo, 'Political Avoidance in Architecture', *Journal of Architectural Education 38 (2)*, 1985, pp18-25; J Habermas, *Communication and the Evolution of Society*, Heineman, London, 1979; See also K Dovey, 'Architectural Ethics: A Dozen Dilemmas', *Architecture*

FROM ABOVE: The forms of participatory process may or may not be radically new but empowerment ensures a renewed depth of meaning. BO 100 apartments, Mälmo, Sweden, 1991 (architect: Ivo Waldhor); the value of architecture is not revealed in the pages of journals but in the everyday life of the places it helps to create – Living with Children project, Vienna (architect: Ottakar Uhl)

Australia, June 1990; K Dovey, 'Feigning the Future: The Politics of Representation in Environmental Design', R Feldman (eds), *Power by Design EDRA 24*, Proceedings, 1993, pp9-13.

15 S Dostoglu, 'On the Fundamental Dilemmas of Architecture as Profession', Faculty of Arch, Middle East Technical University, 1986, pp52-66.

16 D Harvey, 'Flexible Accumulation Through Urbanisation' *Antipode 19*,1987, pp260-286.

17 P Bourdieu, *Distinction: A Social Critique of The Judgement of Taste*, Harvard University Press, Cambridge, 1984.

18 Dickens 'Social Science and Design Theory', *op cit.*

19 The place where you are now, as you finish this paper.

Community collaboration requires more imagination not less – Box Hill Community Arts Centre, Melbourne, 1991 (Architects: Greg Burgess, Kevin Taylor and Maggie Fooke)

MARK WIGLEY
TERRORISING ARCHITECTURE

One way to rethink the old but ever urgent question of 'Power and Architecture' is to think about those who attack power structures by attacking physical structures. The terrorist systematically exposes and exploits our assumptions about architecture. Indeed, the terrorist is by definition a kind of architectural critic.

Terrorism is always a question of space, if not the questioning of space. Its most obvious characteristic is the violation of a space for political ends. A bomb goes off in a crowded bar, shattering the building, the bodies, and the distinction between them. But terrorism is not simply the violation of space. More precisely, it is the possibility of such a violation, since it is usually threatened rather than enacted. A defused bomb can destabilise a political structure just as easily as one that goes off. Indeed, even when it does go off, it is the possibility that it may do so somewhere else that is the agent of instability. Strictly speaking, terrorism is only ever a threat, producing the thought that no part of a space is free of the risk of violence. But not just any part. Terrorism is the attempt to produce the thought that the safest part of a space is unsafe.

The terrorist threat assumes political force inasmuch as it associates the spaces it acts upon with institutions, whether the space be that of a bar, a car, an airliner, a computer network, a power grid, a newscaster's Teleprompter, and so on. Terrorism presupposes the institutional condition of space, putting its violence into some kind of relationship to the violence that maintains that space. It threatens to violate an apparently innocent space in a way that exposes the regime of terror that constructs that space, attempting to provoke a wave of counterterrorism whose violence is seen to exceed its own, and to be part of the everyday constitution of the space. Its victims are randomly selected so that the terrorists can, in the end, identify with them, advertising themselves as victims, protesting the counter-terrorist response by arguing, as Ulrike Meinhof put it, that 'they make us seem what they are.' Protesting, that is, that counterterrorism is not an institutional response to a specific threat but is the underlying structure of the institution that the threat merely exposes.

Given such an overdetermined scene of transference and counter-transference, the relationship between a space and that which seems to terrorise it is complicated, to say the least. Terrorism is at once a strategic threat to institutions and the threat that constitutes institutions as such – there being, in the end, no clear line between institutional and anti-institutional violence, no clear line, for example, between 'state sponsored' and 'anti-state' violence. After all, the word 'terrorism' originated to mark the notorious brutality of the regime with which the French Revolution maintained its supposed virtues of 'liberty, fraternity and equality' between 1793 and 1794. The word's use to describe isolated threats to such a disciplinary order is very new. But the idea of such a threat is clearly not. On the contrary, institutions construct and maintain themselves by opposing that threat. In a way, they construct themselves by constructing the threat. The very sense of space is produced by the sense of what threatens it, of what the space resists, or appears to resist.

An institution does not simply respond to occasional threats to its space. Rather, it constitutes itself as an institution by constantly responding to such a threat through the regulated use of force. The terrorist simply enacts the threat that is already being responded to. Terrorism is therefore a part of what it threatens. It is an institutional phenomenon. Furthermore, all aspects of its theory and practice have become institutionalised, if not professionalised. The rise of terrorist training camps, schools, textbooks, international networks and so on, has been matched by the rise of official think-tanks, government departments, military divisions, academic conferences, national and international legislation, specialised journals, and so on. The interdependency of terrorism and the spaces it haunts has been monumentalised.

Indeed, even more strictly speaking, terrorism does not simply threaten to violate a space. It actually depends, for its effectiveness, on maintaining the limits of the very space it appears to threaten. In the end, it only threatens to expose the violence of that space, but perhaps nothing could be more terrifying than such an exposure. When the security of a space is seen to be the product of the repression of institutional brutality, the victims of 'random' violence can be rendered at once complicitous in a brutal regime and unwittingly terrorised by it. As the attempt to make the violence of a space unavoidable, to make it visible, to publicise or represent it, terrorism is no more than the representation of violence.

The struggle, like all political struggles, is always over representation, in all its senses. Just as the victim of terrorism has to be understood as a representative (no matter how 'innocent'), the terrorist has to be understood as a representative of an organisation which in turn represents a particular cause. What the terrorist attempts to displace is a system of representations, labels that are understood to have the capacity to maim. This includes, of course, the highly contested label 'terrorist', whose successful attachment to an event is typically used to authorise extraordinarily brutal 'counter' operations, to which it might, in turn, be applied. And in this struggle with and over representations, it is not the violence of the 'terrorist' act *per se* that is at stake. After all, even in Northern Ireland, the 'innocent' person is much more likely to be killed in a car accident on the way home than in an exploding bar. It is the particular meaning given to the explosion that counts, a meaning produced and negotiated in the mass media. The bomb is only exploded in the building in order to be seen exploding on the television set. Indeed, telephone calls are often used to ensure that many of the bombs are seen exploding in streets inhabited only by cameras, or defused by sweatless robots whose mechanical eyes do not blink in the face of the lethal mysteries of timing devices – images that seem to make the very threat that is terrorism tangible as such. It is, of course, precisely the development of global media networks that made possible the practice of the terrorist act, the practice whose theory was already there, embedded within the very institutions being assaulted.

But how does architecture participate in this drama (one that no matter how public, is always, in the end, domestic) that is replicating and mutating itself throughout contemporary society? Clearly, it has played an important role inasmuch as the terrorist's sensitivity to the institutional condition of space has been applied to buildings from the beginning. If terrorist acts are always done for the media, a mutilated building is often used as a culturally acceptable (ie broadcastable) image of the mutilation of an institution (whether that institution has any obvious link with that space or not) in the same way that it is used as an acceptable image of mutilated bodies (whether people were killed or not). In this sense, architecture has carried out its traditional

representational function.

But what roles does architecture play beyond this? What is it that terrorises architecture? What is it that torments its traditional representational function? And what is it about architecture that terrorises? Can there be a terrorist architecture? Can you build on terror? What is it that terrorism builds? After all, wasn't the rhetoric of the historical avant-gardes in all the arts the rhetoric of terrorism? And wasn't it echoed, if not exemplified, in the modern architect's call for the 'destruction of the box', the 'explosion of space', and so on, understood as a quasi-military series of isolated incidents in the urban landscape that would eventually mobilise an architectural 'revolution' as a necessary part of a social revolution? Furthermore, since modern terrorism did not begin until the late 60s, is it possible that it models itself after the rhetoric of the avant-garde, rather than the other way around? Perhaps Meinhof's description of her group as 'the self-appointed avant-garde' should be taken quite literally as a reference to the artworld's appropriation and elaboration of paramilitary strategies. Perhaps one of the multiple factors to be taken into account, one that might all too easily be dismissed, is the extent to which the terrorist acts out the fantasies of the artist, invoking all the classic questions of the signature, the ready-made, reproduction, the aesthetics of shock, and so on. At the very least, the terrorist's use of the media needs to be carefully analysed in terms of the avant-garde's extended experiments – raising questions about the seemingly tenuous, yet possibly structural, links between the commodification of the avant-garde and the rise of terrorism.

This would make the already complex relationship between architecture and terrorism infinitely more so. The spaces whose mutilation is so carefully staged as a kind of bloody artwork are often the final product of the very experiments of the avant-garde on which certain key aspects of such performances are tacitly modelled. In an all too familiar story, the pervasive landscape of modern architecture now acts as the media image of the very institutions whose subversion it was supposed to represent. But we need to recall the precise terms of that subversion. Exactly what was being terrorised? For all the radical complication of the relationship between inside and outside that its carefully timed explosions produced, modern architecture in no way interfered with the traditional sense of architecture as that which attempts to locate terror outside, constructing space by domesticating the wild.

Take Le Corbusier, for example. His *When the Cathedrals Where White* analyses the 'adolescent anxiety' that produces the at once advanced and regressive American architecture in a way that makes it clear that architectural shelter is psychological shelter, shelter from terror, as distinct from a shelter that terrorises. He symptomatically interrupts a description of the machine age beauty of jazz to recall that:

> When I flew over the Atlas mountains in a plane, I realised that their formation – through erosion, geological dramas, the action of winds – was completely independent of our moral anxieties; man is in a kind of cyclone; he builds solid houses to protect and shelter his heart. Outside, nature is nothing but indifference, even terror.

Architecture holds terror outside through its 'careful little calculations, as sublime as they are puerile, established in the heart of the tumult'. The book associates the terror of nature with the terror of industrialisation, the 'violent tasks of modern technique' that produce a 'city of horror', an artificial nature that architecture must overcome. But overcome by constructing itself out of the very thing that terrifies, in the same way that jazz defines a new space within the chaotic city by constructing itself out of the 'horrible' sounds of that city, – before transforming that city, it disseminates itself into every home through the radio network, substituting its sound on the interior for that outside the home and literally domesticating the wild sound of the city. For Le Corbusier, jazz is 'more advanced' than the architecture of American skyscrapers. But even its domestication of the industrialised city remains too wild. He goes on to say that he prefers the 'controlled sensuality' of 'the architecture' of Parisian dance hall music, a record of which his wife can admit into the space of their apartment, to the 'hot jazz' of Manhattan. While building itself out of the terrifyingly molten forces of industrialisation, modern architecture must remain cool. The so-called Cartesian skyscraper must calmly, but resolutely, keep out the chaos from which it abstracts itself. It necessarily imposes a 'violent' order, like that of the Manhattan grid, to combat 'violent disorder', but the purity of its form must suppress the 'brutality and savagery' out of which it is constructed. In the city, there is 'so much explosive force in the hard geometry of disordered prisms', and this force must be at once exploited and resisted. While the modern building might be deployed in a terrorist campaign to intimidate classical space, it is only architecture in as much as it resists terror.

Long before we speak of the domestication or commodification of the architectural avant-garde that collapses its terrorist function, we must therefore speak of its own domestication of terror. While adopting the rhetoric of the terrorist, that which terrifies is aestheticised, rendered attractive, stimulating, desirable, and marketed as such. It is not by chance that modern architecture emerges between the wars at the same time as the word 'terrific' starts to assume a positive value, referring, for the first time, to that which pleases as distinct from that which terrifies.

This domestication of terror, which attempts to defend the users of architecture from a threat that is more obviously directed at the architectural profession, is just as manifest in 'post-modern' architectural practices. Denise Scott Brown and Robert Venturi, for example, explicitly formulate their infamous manifestos by claiming that they are using the chaos of the popular vernacular as the new 'horror source' from which an architecture can be shaped, in the same way that modern architects used the industrial vernacular as their's. Architecture yet again accounts for itself as the domestication of terror but now abandons the terrorist rhetoric of the avant-garde at the very moment that this rhetoric has been mobilised in bloody scenes around the world.

More recently, this rhetoric has returned with architectural discourse's engagement with post-structuralist theory, which is itself no more than a rethinking of the historical avant-gardes in the very moment they seem to have lost their force. It is not by chance that this theory exactly parallels the rise of terrorist practices and likewise mobilises the call for a strategic violence that attempts to expose the violence of the apparently benign structures it violates. It is now being deployed to question architecture's capacity to hold terror outside, treating the very effect of space as nothing but the effect of institutionalised suppression of terror by analysing the violence of the very sense of interior, exposing and dissecting the nightmare of space itself that architectural discourse works so hard to suppress and tracking the specific failures of that attempt.

Even while mimicking the avant-garde by tormenting architectural discourse in a terrorist manner, such research does not give rise to the idea of a specifically terrorist architecture. Rather, it suggests that architecture can only ever be built on terror, a terror that can be repressed and displaced but never controlled. Indeed, a terror that is more brutal in its displaced form. In this rethinking of the ancient contracts that bind the architecture of violence and the violence of architecture, avant-gardist militancy gives way to more nuanced reflections, explosions give way to shaking and twisting. Architecture is more under threat than threatening. But while it no longer claims to be ominously ticking, it is even less clear what will happen, where, and to whom. Stay tuned.

POLSHEK

UNITED STATES EMBASSY CHANCERY
Muscat, Oman

A stretch of beach front between the Gulf of Oman and the Hajar Mountains on the eastern end of the Arabian Peninsula provided the site for a diplomatic compound, of which the United States Embassy is a part. A partially covered garden is another significant element. The design responds to functional and security concerns, as directed by the Department of State Office of Foreign Buildings' Operations, and to the rich traditions of Islamic architecture. The result is a functionally efficient, secure and comfortable facility that presents a powerful but consummately diplomatic American presence in this critical, strategic region.

While the building was commissioned in 1980, its programme and design were radically revised in the aftermath of the 1983 bombing of the US Marine Barracks in Beirut and the subsequent upgrading of the Office of Foreign Buildings' security guidelines. Simultaneously, the Sultan issued planning and design guidelines intended to ensure the Islamic character of the public architecture of Oman. Points of entry and service were centralised and window and skylight openings minimised. Surrounded by a mandated ten-foot high wall with one central entry, the building is organised around open and enclosed landscaped courtyards. An exterior, formal entry courtyard and an elaborate rear garden define the front and rear edges of the two-level chancery. For security reasons, the facility is organised into four functional zones: a public zone containing reception lobby spaces; a semi-public area of administrative offices and support services; a private and

secure zone containing offices for military and political personnel and the ambassador's offices; and a high security area housing the communication operations centre. The focus of the chancery is the central atrium space, which filters light into the core of the structure while providing a comfortable and secure gathering place evocative of the region's traditional communal spaces.

The design synthesises two potentially conflicting sources: the structural rationalism and formal asceticism of Modernism as epitomised in the work, of Louis Kahn, and the geometric abstraction and formal richness of traditional Islamic architecture The courtyards and rigorous geometry of the plan, which are devices central to Islamic design, are also remarkably well suited to the functions of the chancery facility.

Structured by quadrangular groups of columns, the serial plan of offices and reception spaces focuses on the central courtyard space. The double perimeter wall system likewise rationalises functional and aesthetic concerns. Composed of an interstitial arcade between a polychromatic stone-clad outer screen wall and a monochromatic tiled inner wall, the wall system affords both sun control and security while the shadows generated by its segmental arches and corner reveals combine with the banded stonework to produce a rich patterning of abstract forms. In its synthesis of indigenous and historic forms with functionally and structurally advanced building systems, the United States Embassy attempts to resolve the dichotomy between formal richness and structural rationalism.

Atrium axonometric; OVERLEAF: Ground Floor Plan; PAGE 49: Section through atrium

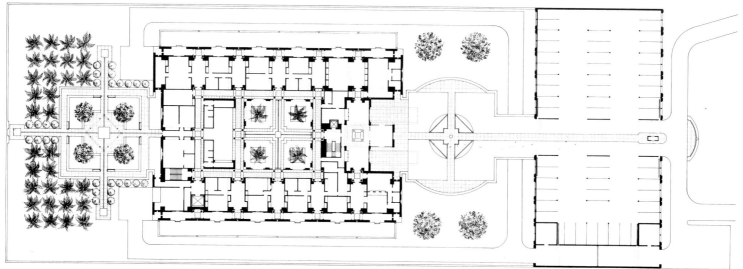

48

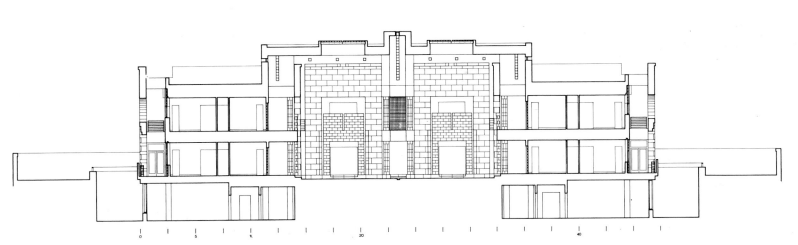

HEIKKINEN-KOMONEN

FINNISH EMBASSY
Washington DC

The new Finnish Embassy in Washington avoids the kind of monumentality that is so common in this type of architecture. However, despite this, the building manages to express far more about its people, and their attitudes, than would have been possible with a more traditional design. The Embassy captures the spirit of the Finnish nation, and communicates their respect for nature, outward reserve and inner warmth.

The restrained modernist exterior conceals a dynamic and stimulating interior, with an almost constructivist aesthetic, that is detailed and finished with an elegance reminiscent of Mies van der Rohe. It is to their credit that the Finnish government have the confidence to commission an understated building rather than an edifice to their greatness.

Essentially, the building is a rigidly geometric, almost minimalist, construction, of glass and green granite, built on a heavily wooded site that falls steeply away towards a small creek. The architects have gone to great lengths to respond to such a beautiful site, both internally and externally, almost to the point where the building appears to merge with the surrounding foliage. The rear and side elevations reflect the lush

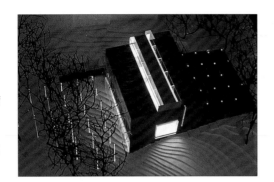

vegetation back at the viewer, whilst at the front the designers have integrated an extruded trellis that will eventually obscure the entire facade behind a wall of climbing plants and flowers. Internally, the glass walls, comprised of a mixture of glazing and glass blocks depending on the amount of privacy required, and the close proximity of surrounding trees work together to blur the distinction between inside and out. There are also other devices employed to strengthen the interior's relationship with the exterior. The modular grid of the building is continued outside of the building, using lights, into the surrounding trees, many on poles to counter the effects of the slope, and across the building's forecourt. Despite its basic geometric form, these features produce the impression of the building reaching out and drawing in both its visitors and environment.

Overall, the quality of the building's design and integration with its site is excellent, yet, this is not the building's true beauty. What makes this building special is that it reminds us that architecture does not need to be monumental to illustrate a nation's identity and that power, either military or political, should not be the only issue worth communicating.

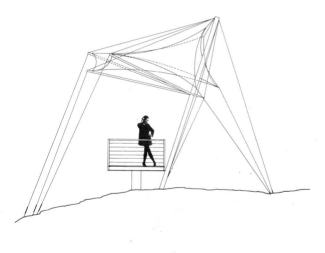

FROM ABOVE: Overview of site model; canopy front elevation; site plan

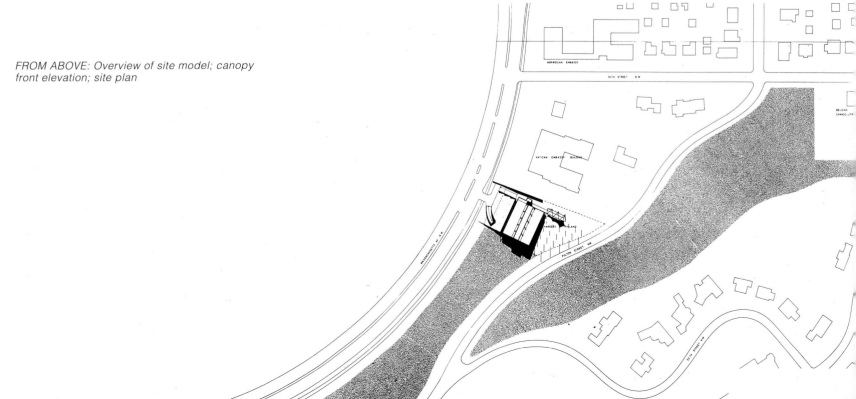

MITCHELL GIURGOLA & THORP

PARLIAMENT HOUSE

Canberra

The achievement of Romaldo Giurgola's design for Parliament House, Canberra, has been questioned by a number of commentators. However, one can be in no doubt, as one emerges from the Great Veranda, onto the paved and mosaic forecourt to look across at the surrounding panorama, of the essentially prehistoric quality of the spatial plan and its elevational conformation of terraces and mounds which address the surrounding landscape of hills and plain and seem to test infinity. While some critics seek references in the work of early German expressionism of the 20th century, the idea of the 'City Crown', and others range as far as St Peter's, Rome, or the Temple at Luxor, it now seems clear that Giurgola's concept is essentially autochthonic; sprung from the land itself. The result is a primordial connotation, and so the references are pre-Columbian and certainly preclassical; and in the first instance, little sociopolitical significance can be read into (far less any religious inference) highway curves, marble halls or anthropomorphic potentialities seen or imagined. Spatially the opening out to the landscape parallels the way in which on emerging from the Central Court at Phaestos in Crete, the mountain landscape is embraced across the plain. To a lesser extent it compares with the disposition of Mycenae to the expanding landscape below, or more formidably it echoes the conditions at Persepolis viewed outwards from the Apadana of Xerxes, as emerging from the audience hall one is confronted by the whole breadth of the plain. There is a striving for the fundamentals of civilisation, yet the discontinuities of history cannot be ignored.

If the Ngunawal people, who were the inhabitants of the plains below the Black Mountain (now within Canberra itself) and who fished the pools of the Murrumbidgee, or Molonglo, thereabouts had survived into the 20th century, they would find little affinity with such aspirations. The only probable point of common ground might be the protein-rich Bogong moth, which today still visits Canberra in springtime, to slide into door crevices or ventilation louvres in shady carparks. If the surrounding hills and lakes of their ancestors appear still to be celebrated, rather than the 20th-century edifices of power, it is presumed nevertheless, that they, too, respect the motto *L'Etat c'est moi*, as appertaining to democracy itself and the logical successor to the king, its own executive body: the obtrusiveness of central government remains and with it the conscious self-aggrandizement of temporal power.

Such were the realities behind the design brief. Of these we must continue to remind ourselves, no less than we might wish to, if facing the sacrificial locations in Mayan cities, or the product of the enslavements of the Pharaohs, Ziggurats or pyramids that we so admire. So indeed, to have experienced this antipodean colossus just before it is finally completed, and prior to the influx of the full apparatus of fixtures and fittings, is by definition to have been provided with what is essentially an archaeological experience. The urge is to disclaim the autochthonous references: but in the nature of things, they tend to recur.

The French philosopher Foucault has made the clear distinction between history, which memorises the monuments of the past and transforms them into documents, and archaeology, a discipline devoted to silent monuments which, as a result, attain new meaning through the recovery of a historical discourse. His point was that in our time history, by contrast, aspires to the conditions of archaeology, transforming documents into monuments. Despite Marx, the epistemological mutation of history is not yet complete, and an explosion of historiography has readily accelerated the manipulation of data. Essentially, with the Parliament House then, we are experiencing an archaeology of the present.

Viewed in October, 1987, the underlying skeletal structure of the whole building was more in evidence than ever, despite occasional obscuration by scaffolding, shuttering and retaining elements. The great curved sweep of the symmetrical side walls was impressive, against the understated elevation of the members' offices. This was substantial in scale, yet an extreme simplicity and clarity in detailing of openings, sills and fenestration overall avoided any charge of monumentality. This again is inherently clean detail design, not the stripped, or phased, classicism so tainted by fascism yet still beloved of post-modernists (cf Venturi's National Gallery Extension, London, 1987). Giurgola in this way expresses the intended accessibility of the building, and such restraint combines to expose the orthogonal ordering of the contents thereby on offer, in an unassuming and unequivocal manner.

This is not, however, a technical critique, and it seems more important here to assess the validity of Giurgola's criteria, and of those imposed by the brief, and hence to review developments in terms of such realities, and the resulting impact all this will have for the future development of Canberra. For one thing is certain, that the city will never be the same again, and that the Parliament House creates inevitable changes, which the still extant plans need to take stock of without delay. However, there have already been considerable departures from the original design of Walter Burley Griffin.

The necessity for a new Parliament Building had been a constant pressure on Australian premiers for years. The 'provisional' Parliament Building had time to settle into the landscape; demolition was soon ruled out, and there was an understandable prevarication about the ultimate siting of the new House. The visiting British architect-planner, William Holford, even proposed a waterside location along Westminster lines, in a 1964 commissioned report negating and reversing the Burley Griffin plan. This was duly abandoned and attempts to reconcile the spirit of Burley Griffin with the message of his successors were made;

ABOVE: Mitchell Giurgola & Thorp sketch from the north of the lake showing the building in the setting of the parliamentary triangle;
BELOW LEFT: Perspective view of Griffin's 1918 design adapted from the 1911 competition entry. The Capitol is at the top of the view with Parliament House in the middle astride the axis;

an apologetic homage *in situ* was ostensibly paid by the distortion of his original concept through the removal of Camp Hill's gradations and the choice of Capital Hill (dismissing his 'Capitol' pretensions), as the final site. Griffin's bicameral Parliament House was to be sited on the now vanished Camp Hill; it was his 'Capitol' that was to rise over this.

The issue of the proposed 'Capitol' and its subsequent dismissal is central to an understanding of the nature and fuller implications of the new Parliament House, but the matter is now seldom aired. This is to be regretted. Burley Griffin considered this building concept to be central to the architectural meaning not only of the parliamentary group, but of all Canberra. That was the philosophical distinction of Griffin's scheme over and above his less successful rivals in the competition for the federal capital of 1911. Eliel Saarinen, the runner-up, proposed that Parliament occupy the higher position, entering a design that incorporated a heightened monumentality with Parliament House in a dominant position. Griffin's Capitol, set on Capital Hill, was not an executive building; instead, it was:

To be a building which is intended to symbolise Australian sentiment, achievement, and ideals, will be used for the housing of archives, etc, and in connection with public ceremonials . . . the building is isolated and centrally focused in an extensive hill park . . . and will by its isolation and the height of its site, 80 feet above the Parliament House, ensure its supremacy as the objective feature, not only of the government group but of the entire city.

An Olympian intention, no less, in the name of the people, and with the mortals of the elected executive confined on Camp Hill below. Yet, was not to be, and Peter Myers is correct in his view that Griffin wanted to emphasise a democratic relationship between the citizens of the new nation, whose identity is symbolised in the capital (and the accessible public surroundings there) and their legislators ensconced in the essentially pragmatic parliamentary chambers designated below. Even the hapless Holford, although he had in his proposal transferred these premises to the lake side, remembered and recognised the aspirations so contained on Capital Hill, and left the idea largely intact, for a national centre there.

This was not to be, and there were further discontinuities in store. Romaldo Giurgola, on winning the Parliament House competition following the second stage assessment in June 1980, had this to contend with and, like Dr Pangloss, he was bound over to accept the best of all possible worlds. Thus, apart from the incorporated revision to site conditions, 1978, and, accordingly, the literal grading out of Camp Hill, in-line with the selection of Capital Hill as the ultimate site, there were clear summaries of intention and expectation from the assessors which emphasised that the new building was to be the 'objective feature' (in an ironic revival of Burley Griffin's usage). As if this were not enough guidance, directives were accompanied by a strong hint as to what might be acceptable in the form of a thumbnail sketch by IM Pei, one of the assessors, reprinted in the official margin. Pei's New York graffiti is a vital clue to the course of events, and Giurgola's eventual winning scheme three months later fits into these quite categorical projections with a minimum of adjustment.

Since those heady days, a number of misconceptions have grown up concerning the extent to which Burley Griffin's ideas, following a difficult period in the 60s and 70s, have by now effectively been 'restored' to fruition. Roger Pegrum, for instance, in an otherwise useful publication on the early development of Canberra claims that 'Burley Griffin would nevertheless be pleased with the design of a fellow American which recognises the Canberra valley and the scale of the Griffin land axis'. It is clear that Griffin would in no way have approved the removal of his 'Capitol' either on philosophical or planning grounds. There is currently a general view that Burley Griffin's plans are back in place, indeed under careful restoration. Certainly it is true that the parliamentary triangle exists, and is recuperating from the questionable design of both the Australian National Gallery and Law Courts, encouraged by the excellence of Lawrence Nield's new Science Centre opposite and supported by new roads and bridges which reinforce the land axis. Also, there is an avowed intention to mark the conjunction of the water axis with the land axis in a manner reminiscent of Griffin's 'Watergate', but this is not exactly restoration.

The fact is that planning in the late 20th Century is increasingly character-ised by the phenomenon of discontinuity. Amendments, departures, executive fashions and budgetary fluctuations all conspire to change. Canberra manifestly is no exception. Both the new and the provisional Parliament buildings, coupled with the discreet removal of Camp Hill, have created a set of circumstances absolutely at variance with the plan, and in particular the sectional gradient and elevation conceived by Griffin. No amount of cotton wool will disguise this, even to the most innocent observer, and if more than a merely archaeological 'truth' is to survive, then the historical mutation must be recognised and arrested.

In the late 20th century, power is manipulated on a global scale to a speed and effect never hitherto experienced, as much by corporations as by nations. Recently, Australian entrepreneurs have entered this global arena successfully, to the benefit of the nation, if not always very noticeably to the advantage of their fellow Australians. The temporal nature of executive power, as operated by a democratically elected federal government, certainly requires to be strengthened as a deterrent to unbridled multinational capitalism – hence emphasis within the new building, on the validity of the nation, on the responsibilities of democracies and the communication of legislation.

Herein lies the dilemma of the Flag. Griffin's Parliament House(s) required no such symbol since the 'Capitol' fulfilled that role, with greater validity as well as less abstractly. Romaldo Giurgola's continuous concern has been with resolving of that symbol *in absentia*. The executive in Parliament has eliminated the 'Capitol' as superfluous, but something must stand for it. Yet even now, it is the least resolved element of the building.

One of the seeming paradoxes of Giurgola's Parliament House is that the building seems most explicit as one moves outwards and northwards from the centre. At the centre lies no marbled basilica (to the evident disappointment of baroque protagonists) but the negation of space, a reflecting pool, a reflected flag. While both flag and reflection are evident there in the neutralised nexus of the Members' Hall, this space contrives an intentional vacuum, even the sound of discussion is carefully muted by the background movement of water.

By contrast, to move from this vacuum of this crossing point, through the Reception Hall, via the Foyer and onto the Great

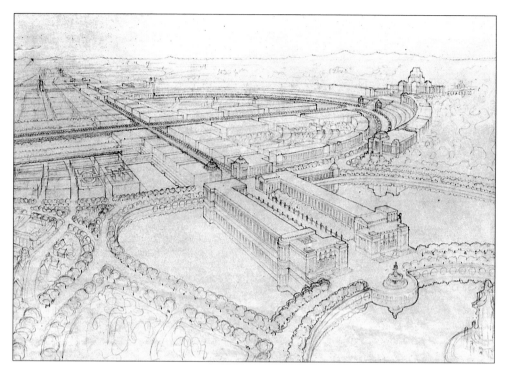

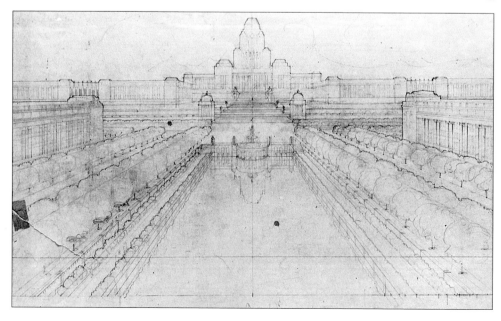

Veranda is to experience a sequential, northward progression towards the sun, that is fundamental to the building's whole design concept. Most impressive of all is the view from the Public Terrace above. Least successful is the Flag, and its superstructure. This is not just a design flaw, a shortfall in one element, but a major failure that springs from the aspects of the site, an abandonment of a philosophy and the contingent discontinuities to which I have referred earlier. Within this paradox lies a further interpretation springing from the limitations of the brief and its incomplete resolution. This architecture, in all its manifest competence, which in certain aspects shows indications of sheer genius, reflects a certain abandonment of discourse. If it carries thus the autochthonic imprint of the future, that too reads from the archaeology rising on Capital Hill.

One resolution of the dilemma of the Flag may be to emphasise the communicative aspect of Parliament. In a media dominated age this can be achieved by realising the superstructure's potential as a telecommunications mast; one senses that in the final analysis Romaldo Giurgola would prefer thereby a programmatic solution to a symbolic gesture of heraldry. However, this is a secondary issue, even an ephemeral aspect, of an otherwise very permanent building, which itself constitutes such a massive intervention within the original plan of Burley Griffin that it virtually rewrites the whole script. Neither, is this a point of criticism in any way, but a recognition of reality, and the story must now offer the lead part to Giurgola.

At about the time that he decided not to be a juror for the competition, but to enter it himself (how many have that degree of commitment) Giurgola was just completing his scheme for the famous *Roma Interrotta* exercise. A number of distinguished architects had been invited to revise and update equal parts of Giambattista Nolli's famous 'New Plans of Rome' completed in 1748. Giurgola, with Hal Guida (also of the Canberra team) and others submitted a project that is significant in any assessment of the subsequent Parliament House project. First, they operated on the plan of Rome with Giurgola essentially an insider, streetwise in his native city, alive to the ordering of design and social policies in that most gregariously proletarian of cities. Giurgola indeed supplied a fundamentally social programme. He examined the prevailing circumstances existing at the impoverished edge of the city, and pursued urban 'interventions' at the most pragmatic level, generating new structures along the Aurelian Walls. This periphery was to be transformed programmatically into a receiving zone or transit campus for migrants.

At the Porto San Lorenzo a place of expectation will be built, both an inn and a training place . . . where whoever wants to emigrate to the city will stay a while to learn about its life.

Visually this was to mediate between urban and agrarian life, exploring their separate contingencies to a degree comprehensible only if one realises that Giurgola's own experience as a migrant from the 'country' of the world to the city of New York lay behind the scheme.

So, in Rome, Giurgola rendered propositions that seek, to authenticate in form and content the inherent and timeless landscape of Latium outside the city walls (as per Nolli) as an essential precedent to urban definitions. In place of a supposed modernist determinism we find a revisionism of manifold reference; socially too, a characteristic embrace of the Roman 'populus' autochthonous, agrarian, proletarian.

So now we recognise, closer to home, what is essentially Canberra *Interrotta*. The 'intervention' posed by the Parliament House is of a wholly different dimension, and built in a social and economic context inconceivable to Burley Griffin. There are corresponding ramifications, not just for the concept and future location of a proposed National Archives building (the current one being apparently stillborn), but for the future scenario along the lake. Indeed there might be a positive dichotomy between the Parliament Building and the embryonic idea germinating in Canberra for a lake side National Museum of Australia. Meanwhile the general consensus suggests an overdue period of recuperation for the Parliamentary Triangle following the completion of Parliament House and the welcome addition of the Science Centre below. While it is true that Burley Griffin's Canberra will never be the same again, such changes largely predate the Parliament Building, whose own brief stemmed from earlier considerations. As such, designed water and landscaping, with the insertion of both formal and informal gardens, plus a forthright reappraisal of the conjunction of the land and water axes, as construed in Burley Griffin's Watergate, seems desirable, given the possibility of waterborne traffic and a tourist influx beyond expectations. While Burley Griffin's 1912 plan postulated closely related, formalised relationships for buildings within the Parliamentary Triangle, facing down to the lake – north facing buildings, orthogonally disposed with colonnades, verandas, sun screens, salient in the clear light, predominated over landscaping that was essentially ancillary. Now, conversely, below the autochthonic mound conceived by Giurgola, terrain must predominate over built form. Just as the lake itself is now only partially visible over the roof of the Provisional Parliament, from the Great Veranda of the new building, so this intervention, and the spasmodic nature of earlier architecture below has opened up the formality of the lake to new possibilities.

The mute reflection of the Flag in the pool of the Members' Hall might be the starting point for something big, more than a spotlit flagpole, a whole new game of lake side illuminations. Giurgola, in Canberra *Interrotta*, could be drawing us back to the fundamentals of civilisation, the Bogong moth would probably be the first to agree, heading down to the lights.

Michael Spens

OPPOSITE, FROM ABOVE: Eliel Saarinen, Town Planning Scheme for Canberra, general perspective, 1912; Parliament Building perspectives

PI DE BRUIJN
DUTCH PARLIAMENT SECOND CHAMBER
The Hague

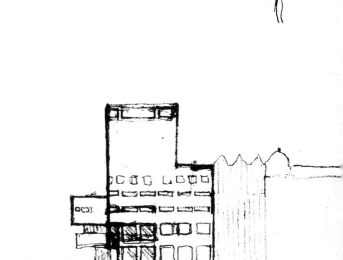

With any process spanning more than a few years, the changing spirit of the times left its mark on the new Second Chamber buildings. In retrospect, several points deserve a mention. Over the last decade, there has been a conspicuous change in ideas on openness, privacy and status. The original programme of requirements for the competition in 1977 emphasised the need for the Chamber building to be 'open' to the city and the public. However, the Chamber is perhaps one of the institutions least likely to ignore the calls of recent years for tighter security against aggression, vandalism and terrorism.

The Chamber's request for the relationship between the plenary hall and the environment to be emphasised, and for the halls to be open to a wider public, unmistakeably found a satisfactory response in De Bruijn's design. However, the architect originally planned the central hall as a passageway from the Hofcingelplein to the Plein, which would make it an integral part of the public area. Visually, this transparency has certainly been achieved but, in fact, the hall can now be reached only after thorough security checks. An electronic pass system separates access for the users and the public. In better times, however, this technical device could be reversed by the press of a button.

The greater need for privacy, combined with revived status consciousness, is also reflected in other ways. In one of the restaurants, a private section has been reserved for MPs, which was not the intention in the programme of requirements. Now MPs enjoy a waiter service in this area, while in the early 80s, the plan was for full self-service.

A more far-reaching change was the Chamber's wish that every MP should have his own room. The final programme of requirements was based on 18 m² per MP (comparable to the space allotment for a senior civil servant such as a Lieutenant Colonel at the Defence Ministry or the Mayor of a small municipality). However, the planned combination of

rooms with personal and party workers, was no longer wanted. In view of the limited space available in the old buildings, the Government Building Agency (RGD) is assiduously seeking a solution in the form of future expansions in the area around the Binnenhof.

The renewed demand for more formal relations also had an influence in the Chamber's rejection of the statue by Kounellis on the Hofcingelplein. The earthy symbolism of 'fossilized energy' (coal packed in steel) was apparently too direct. There were also contemporary issues, such as the request of female MPs for their own tunnel from the new building to the car park on the Plein, for safety reasons, or the requirement of the City of The Hague for the height of the press tower to be reduced. In the changing climate of the 90s, a higher building was more likely to have been welcomed. Nevertheless, there has been remarkable unity and continuity in the progress during the past decade.

Certainly in comparison with all the consternation caused by the competition and the multiple assignment at the end of the 70s, the design and construction process proceeded almost without a hitch in the 80s. The confused and often emotional discussions in the preliminary stages seem ultimately to have clarified and organised the issues. Slowly but surely, from a multitude of possibilities and unclear programme requirements, a concept was developed which was able to convince everyone.

A number of reasons can be given for this. From the conceptual point of view, the otherwise disastrous competition in 1979 was of major importance. The controversial submission by Rem Koolhaas had a shock effect. The simplicity and clarity of his design (two office axes of equal width, standing square to the old Binnenhof complex and linked by the plenary hall) was revolutionary in a period when the guiding principles in architecture were small-scale buildings, intimacy and variety. The comments in the jury

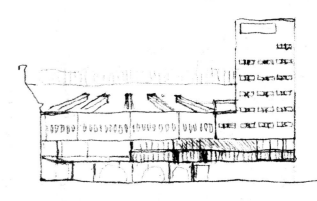

FROM ABOVE: Initial sketch – preliminary mass studies; initial sketch – Lange Poten facade; initial sketch – Hofplaats Facade; initial sketch – The New Chamber

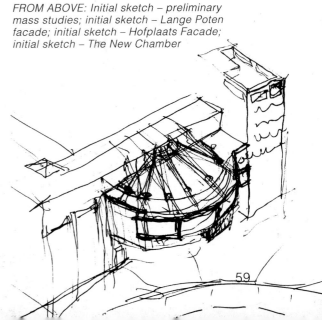

report speak volumes on this point: 'a hard plan', 'manipulation', 'the area will be ruined', 'the users are subordinated to his formal vision'.

The importance of Koolhaas' approach perhaps lay less in his design itself as in the fact that it set new ideas in motion, not only for the design of the Second Chamber, but in Dutch architecture as a whole. Koolhaas instigated a new climate in Dutch architecture and town planning, which certainly contributed to the choice of De Bruijn in the multiple assignment and his subsequent selection in 1980.

Koolhaas' influence, which De Bruijn has frequently acknowledged in public, can clearly be seen in his submission for the multiple assignment: particularly, in the North-South axis on the Binnenhof. Yet, De Bruijn says he was also largely inspired by Berlage's work, including

both the Amsterdam Stock Exchange building (handling large building volumes in an urban context) and the facade of Meddens' shop on the Hofweg, opposite the new Second Chamber (the metropolitan, 'un-Dutch' feel). Furthermore, the De Bruijn plan was not purely a conceptual exercise, but the result of an intensive analytical process. This analytical work formed the basis for the ultimate choice of De Bruijn as the architect, against the tide at the time, by the government architect, the RGD and the Cabinet.

The analytical preparatory work also proved to be of major importance for the rapid progress made in the subsequent research and design process. The Chamber's unclear, contradictory and sometimes exaggerated programme requirements were made comprehensible and the options were broken down into

digestible parts. In addition, intensive consultation, between the architect, RGD and all parties concerned, in the research phase meant that close mutual understanding and trust developed. After the research phase, there were virtually no further conflicts with the Building Supervision Committee (BBC) over requirements. This gave the architect scope to realise his own ideas, which would otherwise have been considerably more difficult. Undoubtedly, his (diplomatic) experience as a former official of the Amsterdam Housing Department and as project leader of the Bijlermeer building, which was a *tour de force* in processing terms, also contributed towards the success of the design process. De Bruijn also had two years' experience as an architect in urban development and housing design in London and had realised an urban

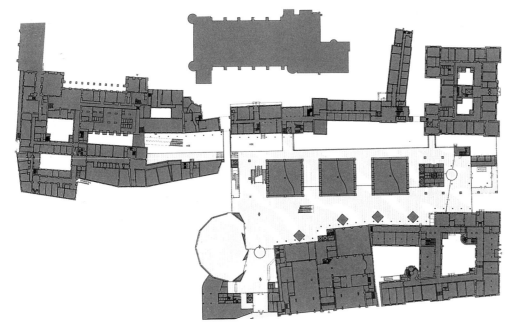

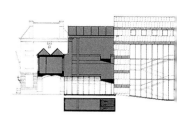

renewal project in Amsterdam.

More important than rapid progress, although this was the main aim for the Chamber, was the impact of the preliminary analysis on the quality of the design itself. It allowed the number of square metres to be reduced, the planned area to be expanded, the premises along the Lange Poten to be retained and also provided support for the decision to demolish the Supreme Court building. Another important effect was that no surprises were faced while construction work was in progress. Generally speaking, the work kept within the original (index-linked) budget. Additional work in one area was compensated in others. The tight control exerted by the project leader, and the architect's flexibility, certainly contributed towards this too.

The interesting point about the final design is that it is in fact no longer a 'new' building in the usual sense of the word. The office space is all included in the old surrounding buildings and, to a much lesser extent, in the press tower. The central hall serves far rather as an organising principle or 'binder' for a wide variety of buildings with different functions and styles, ranging from functionalist to Dutch Renaissance. The new building holds only a few blocks of meeting rooms, public areas, passageways and, of course, the main hall.

In fact, something paradoxical happened during the preparation and design process. The 'formal autonomy' of the design in the multiple assignment plan, which was so warmly welcomed by the government architect, evolved into a structure in which new and old buildings form an integrated whole. This structure is emphasised by the use of granite in a colour which suggest continuity between the interior and exterior of the building. De Bruijn has thereby completed the formerly fragmented Binnenhof complex and integrated it with the city. The outcome of ten years of planning and design is that the Binnenhof and Second Chamber form more of a unity than ever with the royal residence.

L TO R: Ground Floor Plan; New Chamber first floor plan; BELOW, L TO R: Sectional elevation towards existing buildings; Hofplaats facade; Lange Poten facade

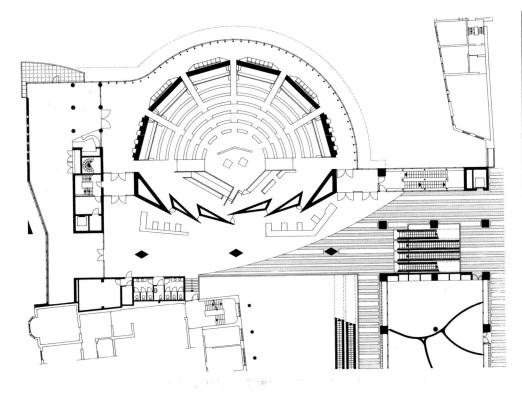

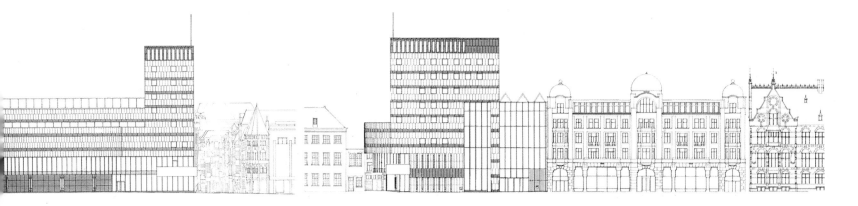

SIR NORMAN FOSTER

REICHSTAG
Berlin

Represented here are Foster's competition stage design, submitted in October 1992, and a version of his modified winning scheme of June 1993. In the earlier design, which was placed first along with Calatrava and Pi de Bruijn, Foster created a distinctive canopy to cover the shell of the building and placed it on a granite plinth. He wrote: 'The shell of the old Reichstag is an historical foil to the new, as well as providing environmental layering . . . The transformation of the Reichstag is about light and lightness,

using materials with related values which are opposite but complementary.

The scheme guts the Reichstag of Paul Baumgarten's internal arrangement from the 1960s and reinstates the first three floors of the historical building and its light wells. The Assembly is placed symbolically at the building's heart beneath the site of the old dome, with circulation for politicians and public in the podium. By the second phase, however, the canopy has been discarded.

We do not recommend raising this roof

artificially above the skyline of the present building – either as a new dome or a version of our original umbrella. To do so poses no technical problems beyond that of further cost . . . however, at a philosophical level we question the need for purely symbolic purposes, of going higher than necessary and spending more money for questionable effect.'

BELOW: Competition scheme, section; intermediate scheme, sectional perspective

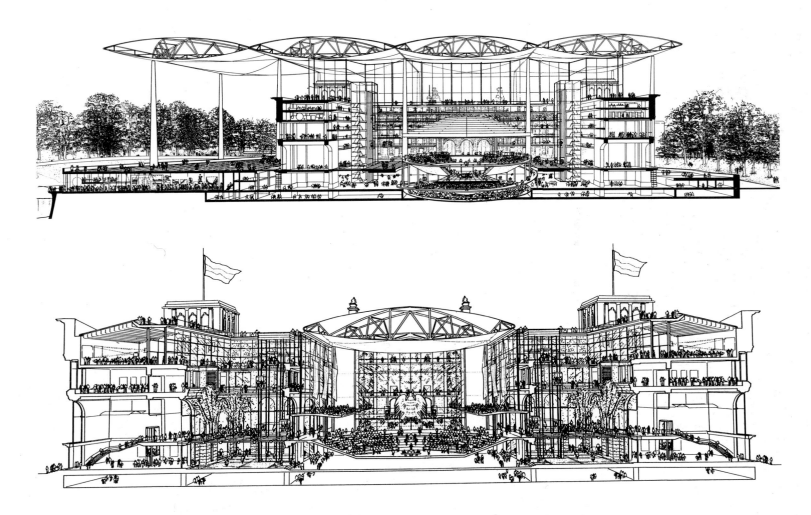

63

SANTIAGO CALATRAVA

REICHSTAG
Berlin

The organisation of the Reichstag competition was problematic from the start. The brief was criticised for its lack of information on the circular assembly hall stipulated and the amount of office space required.

Calatrava's scheme was one of only two to include a dome, a dome of large segments which could be opened upwards, their bases pivoting on the gallery edge. Calatrava wrote:

> The main statement made by the design is to be found in the development of a new space, an appropriate setting for the representation of the people . . . The substance of the original Reichstag building remains and encloses the new structure . . . The four corner towers, together with the massive, original structure will be left, and the facades will remain as Wallot intended. The building will thus retain its identity. A new inner life, and therefore a new meaning for contemporary dome construction . . . The assembly hall receives daylight through an 18-metre opening in its ceiling.

The jury praised Calatrava's scheme as intelligent and elegant: 'the organisation is in harmony with the highest architectonic spatial and planning quality'. Confusion continued, however, with two other schemes also awarded first place, and the whole competition being criticised for its poor timing – many believed that it should have been organised after and not simultaneously with the Spreebogen master plan competition. One month later the three winning practices were asked to re-submit their proposals to take into account amended specifications which included use of space in the adjacent Dorotheen block to the east, and the orientation of the assembly hall with the presidential building on the eastern side – both ideas originally conceived by Calatrava.

Though several of Calatrava's bold proposals had already caught the City's imagination, he was not selected to execute the rebuilding of the Reichstag.

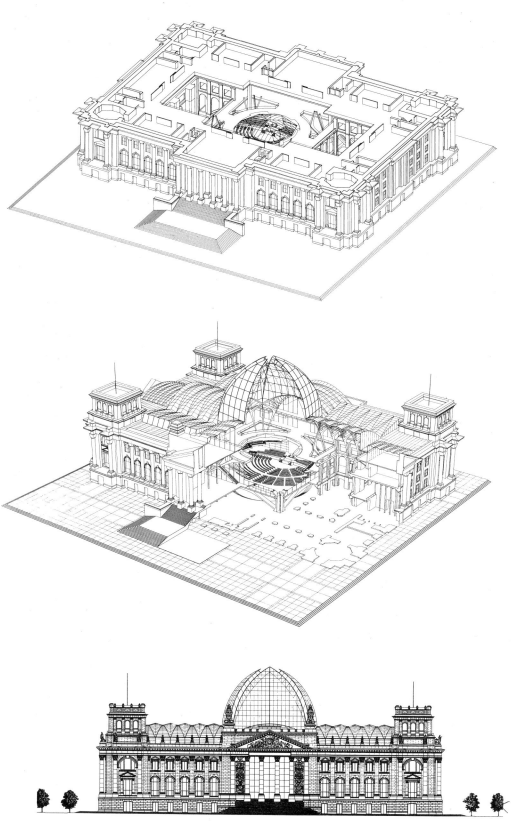

FROM ABOVE: Sectional axonometric; cut-away axonometric; front elevation

JEAN NOUVEL AND EMMANUEL CATTANI

REICHSTAG
Berlin

The Reichstag invokes respect, witness both to the workings of the German Assembly and then to darker times and bitter lessons. We propose to make the Reichstag a place of remembrance, a memorial . . . It will become the noble and historical entry to the new parliament, a place for protocol, and a space where reflection upon fundamental political topics can be performed in serenity . . . [In the design of the parliament] the real task is to symbolise evolution through a new architecture which takes into account both an irrevocable past and a future, hopefully secure and solid, which looks forward to idealistic values. We propose to build a 'double', a twin to the existing Reichstag, as a modern working place for elaborating the laws of the nation . . .

The parliament exploits all the potential of the site. Located along the Spree, it assumes its symbolic dimensions and embraces its whole territory. As a dominating feature of a most beautiful park, it must remain the focal point by discarding the buildings of small architectural interest which spoil its neighbourhood. It must quietly claim its territory, generous in symbols and quality of life for its users and visitors . . . By their nature, institutions require symbols. The sphere of the assembly is one of them: precisely located, perfectly shaped. It glows in the middle of the garden under the protection of the civil servants and representatives of the nation.

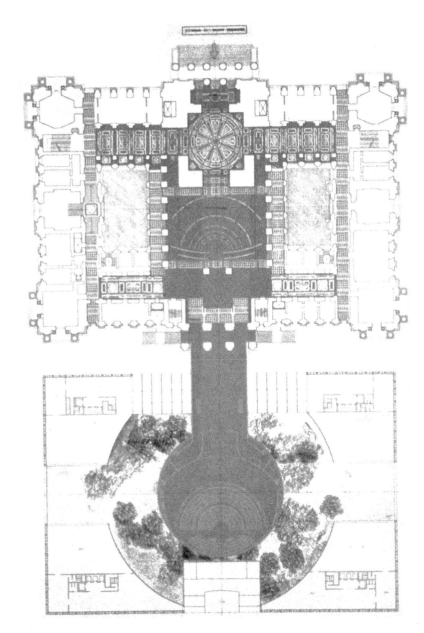

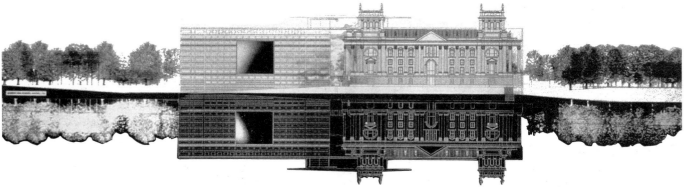

FROM ABOVE: Plan; front, side and rear elevations

COOP HIMMELB(L)AU

REICHSTAG
Berlin

We wish to clearly show present political
conditions. The concept of the building
reflects the simultaneity of diverse points
of view within democratic systems – old
and new structures have equal value.

A new, appropriate form recognises
both the new as well as the former
functions of the Reichstag, presenting
democratic methods for making decisions
. . . A media facade (directly integrating
the media with the building) brings
political news to a wide public. The four-
year 'egg timer' clock in the assembly
hall implies that one could take part in the
activities in the interior. A cross section
along the east-west axis provides a
'setting free' of the southern part of the
building – it should be completely reconstructed and function as a monument.

The building still faces in the east-west
direction of the Platz der Republik. The
public entrance to the west is supported
by the media facade, and a new entrance
to the west leads to the presidential wing.
A further entrance facing north reflects
developments on the Spreebogen. The
assembly hall combines the old and the
new – two bridges link this structure to
the old building and are themselves signs
of the new. The organisational concept of
the functions is allied to the inner form.
The press tower may be seen as transforming interior into exterior.

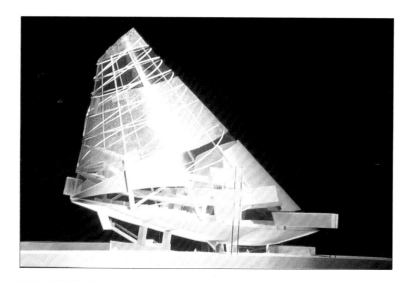

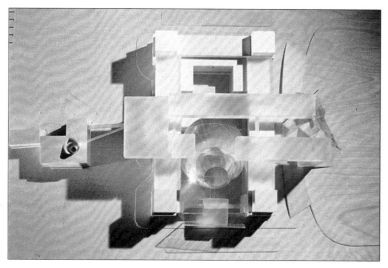

Views of model

GOTTFRIED BÖHM, PETER BÖHM & FRIEDRICH STEINIGEWEG

REICHSTAG
Berlin

With this scheme the architects were keen to stress that the reconstruction of the Reichstag as the new Bundestag should respect Wallot's existing structure, while acknowledging the need for reconsideration of the centre of the building. They also felt it important that, with the new spirit of democracy so stressed in the Spreebogen brief, the building should be integrated into the city fabric, a connection stressed by the presence of bridges which connect to neighbouring buildings.

The building is completely open on the ground floor, being utilised and understood both as a parliament and a house for the people. Thus the entrance zones in the east and west, as well as the auditorium, are opened up to the public for information and discussion, much like a large covered agora within the city structure.

The assembly hall is situated immediately above this public zone, marked by the striking form of an interlocking dome. The interplay of its various shell-like elements, with their penetrating, individual shapes and articulated movements, present a unified body. The constructive leaves are designed so that every layer is made up of visible steel ribs which reciprocally stabilise each other, emphasising the protective effect of the shell. The whole combines to produce a strong visual image for the centre of the German Parliament.

FROM ABOVE: Explanatory sketch of dome and chamber; conceptual study of facade; computer-generated image of dome

ALSOP & STÖRMER

HÔTEL DU DÉPARTEMENT DES BOUCHES DU RHONE
Marseilles

An architecture of power is inherently manifest, by definition, in those buildings which historically are conceived in order to house the executive of power, and by extension the instruments of power, whether temporal or spiritual. In this instance it might be useful to draw some comparisons on an historical basis. In 1994 the completion of the Hôtel du Département des Bouches du Rhone, Marseilles, by the British architect Will Alsop, provided a remarkable example of the architecture of power, where the architect, following a protracted competition saga in 1990, interpreted a set of explicit requirements of a wholly constructional and practical definition on the one hand, while at a different level of interpretation has distilled a largely unwritten perception of basic precepts both of a social, and also a political nature.

At the press airing of *Le Grand Bleu* (as the vast blue enterprise was soon christened by the Marseilles public), Jean Millet, director of L'Institut Francais d'Architecture claimed that:

L'Hôtel du Département 13 est avec L'Arche de la Défense, une des réalisations majeures de la France du 20ème siècle, et même de l'Europe. Non seulement pour la qualité et le modernisme de son architecture, mais aussi pour la qualité des préstations et l'usage nouveau de la couleur dans un bâtiment de béton.

In this announcement is revealed the key to the existence of the building; firstly a statement of regional identity, for the region, as opposed to Paris, as epitomised here by the massive L'Arc de la Défense, and simultaneously an affirmation that *Le Grand Bleu* at least must aspire to the top rank of architectural quality, in an explicit gesture of '*le modernisme*'. Here too lies the dilemma, succinctly put by Milan Kundera: 'Until now progress has always been thought of as a promise of something better. We know now that it announces the end.'

Against this doomsday sentiment, architects (in the position in which Alsop

found himself with such a commission) have constantly had to grapple with an enlightened but powerful client, to break out. Never has this been so difficult as it has in the last two decades. *Le Grand Bleu* illustrates how a dedicated, even ingenious, talent can turn the tables.

Today, civic architecture is as power conscious as it has ever been. The values which new regional, urban, or metropolitan centres must enshrine reflect the universal franchise upon which executive, constitutional power has to seek election and re-election. In Marseilles, the Hotel du Département houses the chamber of government, together with a significant, yet ultimately changeable *cadre* of administrators and bureaucrats.

One major priority here was the incorporation, in the building, of manifestations of what in French is called *conscience*. This is best translated as consciousness, or social awareness, dependent upon the continued existence of social values in the execution of this power, and specifically those community values cherished in France, yet which were so peremptorily to be jettisoned in Thatcher's England. Such *conscience* emerged as clearly explicit in the building of *Le Grand Bleu*. Alsop, the architect, realised that success or failure depended on the degree to which he could effectively mediate such aspirations by the client within the broader cultural field prevailing locally; in such a way as to prove acceptable broadly to the electorate of the region, and yet confound the prophets of doom and the enemies of progress. Not an easy task to pursue in the city of Marseilles.

In 16th-century Florence there stands, fully evident today, a remarkable comparison to this, achieved on behalf of the all powerful Cosimo de Medici (Cosimo I) by the architect Giorgio Vasari. What is interesting is that, although the client was effectively an absolute ruler, the ingredients confronting the architect were identical in composition. The Palazzo Vecchio, of course already existed as the

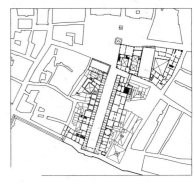

FROM ABOVE: Palazzo Vecchio, Galleria degli Uffizi, courtyard; atrium view with 'Ovoid'; Palazzo Vecchio, Galleria degli Uffizi, upper floor plan

established Florentine seat of executive power. However, the adjacent administrative buildings which Vasari designed, and linked with it, follow an almost identical structural relationship to that established by Alsop.

At Marseilles, the accommodation is broken down into distinct parts by Alsop. Two parallel blocks, the *Administratifs* for obvious reasons, create *per se* an internal, atrium space or *Place de Ville* running North-South. Linked to this inherently logistical complex is, the visually distinctive, *Deliberatif*, a cigar-shaped building of a largely constructivist aesthetic which exudes the semblance of executive, proactive, importance. It so happens that short, upper level bridges link the two major elements together. In the case of Vasari's Uffizi, the link is provided by a single, upper-level enclosed bridge, but the connectivity of executive power with administration, its mechanics, and its servicing function, is equally unmistakable in both cases. The difference, significantly, is that the 16th-century Florentine public was largely excluded from this connection, while in the 20th century it is maintained specifically as the visible means of contact and accessibility, between not just the administration, but also the public, and the executive

In Vasari's day the Uffizi constituted a wholly new building type – such buildings for bureaucracy, tax inspectors and commercial counsellors (city guilds) had not existed. The twin parallel galleries to house these functionaries, gathered up by edict from all over Florence into one space, faced each other across a void, a tangential axis that, whether brilliantly or fortuitously, was not closed at its conjunction with the river Arno: the transparent Loggia dei Lanzi linking the two blocks at the end, (and by egress onto a pedestrian system ultimately linking up with the Pitti Palace via the Ponte Vecchio) revealed clear sky, the Arno river and the hills beyond the far bank.

Vasari's whole architectural reputation (since he was a rare combination of impresario, writer, painter and architect) rests on his definition, and mediation, of

this new typology, and its impact on the Florentine townscape. The offices (Uffizi literally) served to enhance the temporal power of the Medici rulers residing in the Palazzo Vecchio, supreme and unchallenged: The Uffizi being graced with an elementary but absolutely unclimacteric facade of considerable elegance, comprised a dramatic two-point perspective which focused on the transparent loggia, and the clear blue beyond. Through this 'serliana', (functioning as a kind of mediation, phenomenal and transparent) can be contemplated the uninterrupted extension, even extrusion of power. Probably the actual design was not actually by Vasari, but by Bartolomeo Ammanati working under him, but surely it is an insertion of genius.

At Marseilles, it is a reasonable presumption that the transparent ovoid insertion into the atrium, at the southern end, of *Le Grand Bleu*, is by Alsop; it could not be otherwise. It closes the extruded two-point perspective of the atrium, between the two blocks which comprise the *Administratif*. The result is a mediation that is remarkably similar to that of the Vasari Loggia. Likewise, at Marseilles, the conjunction at midpoint of the eastern *administratif* block, with the *Deliberatif* is wholly dramatic.

The only major difference is that at Marseilles the conjunction is congenial, even convivial. There is a disarticulation in the underlying relationship and connectivity of parts, a degree of informality, a mediation of the effects of power, which seems on balance to strike the right note of negotiability between the overtaxed electorate and their over-stressed elected representatives in government. Just as Vasari was concerned with the continuation, undiminished of the Renaissance 'project', so has Alsop been undeniably committed to the survival of the 'modern', albeit in amended form. In this evolved 'modernism' there is evident fulfilment in the manner in which such treatment moderates the exercise and pursuit of the executive power of the client. Here, the monumentalism of *Le Grand Bleu* is ostensibly disavowed or dislocated: such

traditional manifestations as the canopies on the *Deliberatif* emphasise this (the aviary of multicoloured birds intended for the southern elevation has not materialised, but was proposed to the same purpose). Likewise, Alsop wished for greater public access to restaurant and cafeteria spaces and their terraces, not all of which has been allowed. Alsop's urge to achieve a public mood of conviviality has nonetheless been fulfilled at Marseilles, inherently carrying out the original brief.

Thus we find that in confronting, interpreting and defining the exercise of power and its expression through building, architects are obliged to resolve the problem posed effectively by an act of mediation, whereby both the source of power, and those over whom the power is exercised, are both explicitly acknowledged in such a relationship as thus evoked and harmonised through architecture. It is interesting that such fundamentals have not significantly altered over four and a half centuries. The bridge which Vasari created between the Palazzo Vecchio and the Uffizi offices, and the bridges linking Alsop's *Deliberatif* with the *Administratif* blocks, symbolise the same essential relationship between the executive and the functionaries. The public space between the two parallel Uffizi blocks, and the drawing out of the eye via the loggia to the blue beyond, is a historic precursor to the atrium space created by Alsop between his administrative blocks: with its reliance on the ovoid at the southern end, establishes that similar conditioning transparency for the Provençal public, to valid purpose. In each case the architect of power has grasped his essential role, to mediate between identity and the image of power, and its perceived extent. For this reason Alsop's apparent mode of disengagement and informal linkage between parts (bridges at many points) coupled with such devices as a podium level sloping gently towards the entrance lobby, is highly effective in embodying the resonances of a democracy as yet unanticipated by Vasari in 1560.

Michael Spens

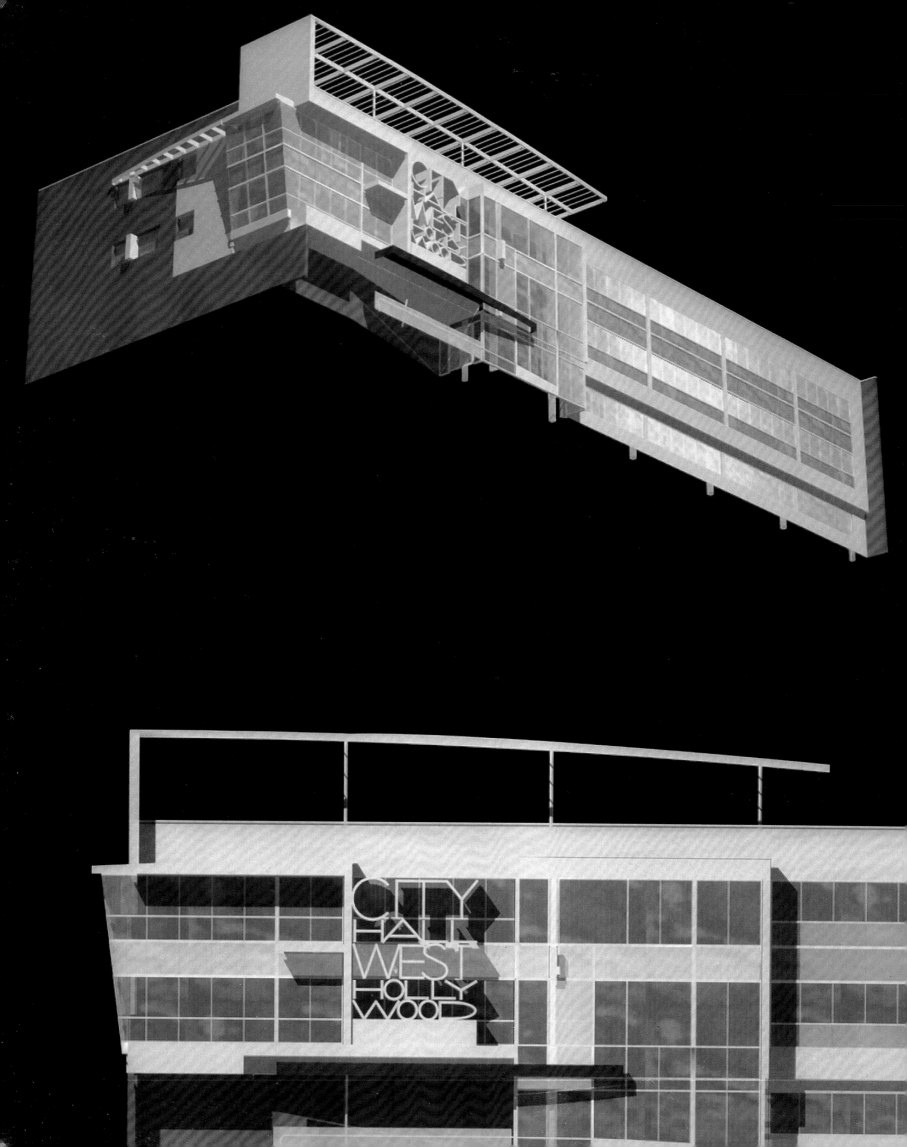

MEHRDAD YAZDANI – ELLERBE BECKET
WEST HOLLYWOOD CITY HALL
LOS ANGELES

This project, currently under construction, is an adaptive conversion of a 34,000 square foot commercial office building into the new West Hollywood City Hall. The new programme entails a public lobby, community meeting rooms and a consolidated set of office spaces for all city departments.

Transformation of the nondescript commercial building into an expressive, individualistic civic identity was considered the primary challenge. Formal and structural interventions are integrated with the existing structure to create a series of 'signs' lending the building a more suitable presence. The primary element is the painted steel canopy atop the building that alters the profile of the building from its surroundings. Below it is a two-storey tilted window wall with translucent and clear glass panels that emphasises the corner and connects the north and east facades. The principal expression of the north facade is a three-storey glass volume framed in clear adonized aluminium. This volume sup-

ports a red cantilevered canopy that signals the entrance to the public lobby.

The buildings' internal focus is a two-storey atrium cutting through the glass box that visually links the lobby to the second floor public service counter. All of the interventions serve not only to integrate the building with its site but also to represent the status and use of different parts of the building. The total effect of all the parts is to lend the building a visual and metaphorical presence in the urban landscape.

OPPOSITE AND OVERLEAF: Computer- generated renderings; ABOVE: Freehand perspective by Mehrdad Yazdani

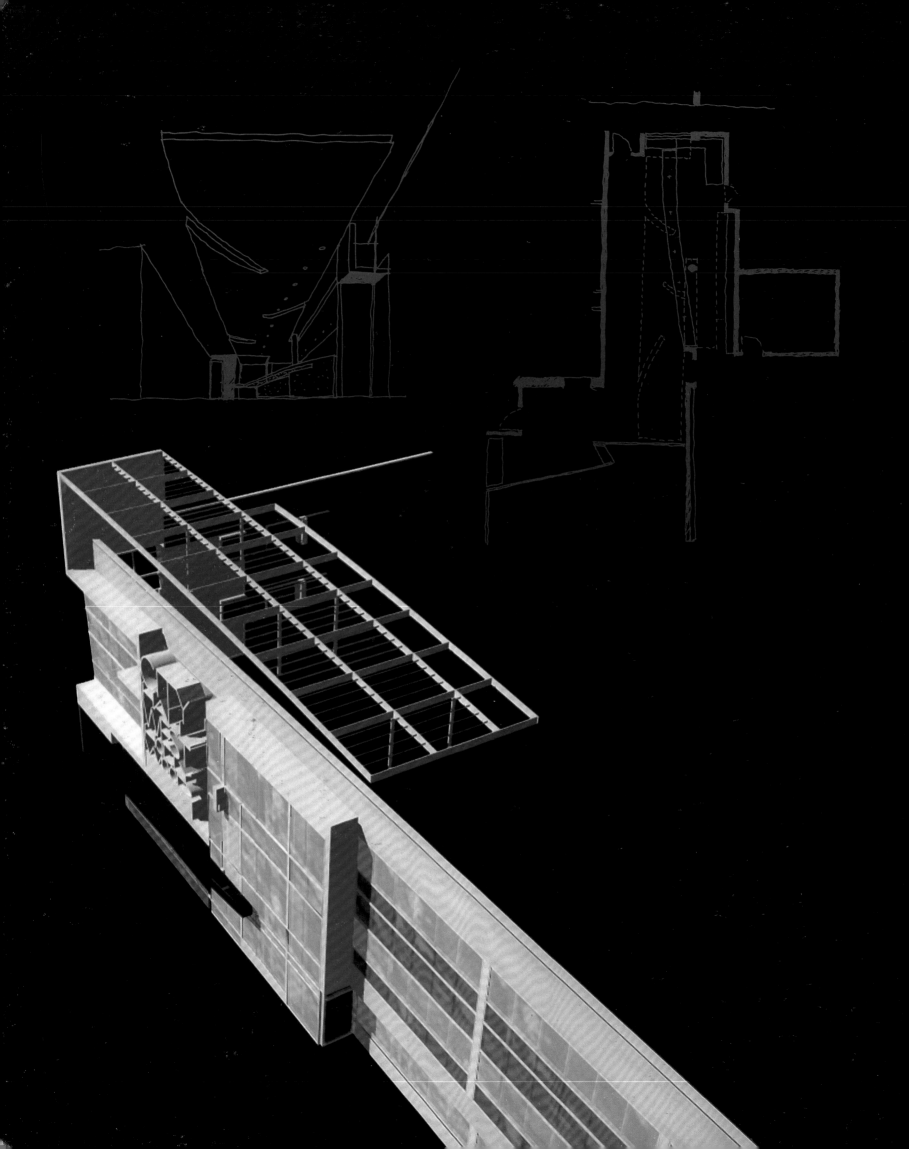

DWORSKY
MUNICIPAL COURTS FACILITY
Los Angeles

The award winning Van Nuys Municipal Court, completed this year and designed by Robert Rosenberg of Dworsky Associates contains 23 courts, and is part of Los Angeles' $500 million courthouse construction scheme. Despite the internal morphology, which reflects the strict functional hierachy and complex zoning requirements defined in the brief, externally, and in the public areas, the architecture possesses a spatial freedom that is refreshing in legal architecture.

This openness is achieved through a number of factors. In particular, the facade, contained within an authoritarian granite surround, is a ten-storey wall of glass that opens the internal spaces up to the public on the street outside. This welcoming, rather than intimidating, architectural approach is further stressed by the three-storey glass block rotunda that projects into the street, reaching out and embracing the public. The finishes within these public areas were also chosen to lighten the oppressive atmosphere within, choosing low maintenance Formica rather than a more traditional heavier granite. This Formica is even continued into the courtrooms themselves which are located on the third floor. Only the areas reserved for the judges, barristers and court officials are lined with mahogany, underlining the power structures within the legal profession.

Since its opening the building has been a great success, with both employees and the public finding its architecture user-friendly rather than authoritarian. It is generally agreed that courthouse architecture should move away from the intimidating buildings of previous generations, and that it should reflect societies' new and supposedly enlightened views on crime and punishment. The elegant, almost corporate facade, of this building does not appear to communicate the nature of the building. Apart from a variety of portentous inscriptions within, 'Justice Is The Sum of All Moral Duty', there is little to lead one to believe that this is actually a courthouse.

REMY BUTLER
MAISON D'ARRET
Brest, France

This prison in Brest opened its doors in 1990 to accommodate 220 inmates, consisting of men, women and young offenders, for short term detention.

The severe austerity of the exposed concrete walls evokes harsh associations, yet is a significant contrast to the interior which is designed to encourage communication, rather than effect sensorial privation so often induced by the traditional penal model. Enclosed within the sculptural mass are the social and medical places, gymnasium, laboratories, general housing, courtyards, sportsground, and cultural facilities. Administration, storage, semi-liberty area and parlours are located outside this area.

At Brest, the psychological quality of life of the inmates has been taken into consideration, initiating a spatially stimulating environment that is filled with light and colour wherein the confined inmates can move about with more freedom. Bright colours are applied to surfaces throughout the building, for example in activity areas, service facilities, columns, doors and details; the cell interiors are of a lighter, softer tone that is accentuated by colour features.

This monumental building is positioned in a north-south direction which serves to exploit fully the qualities of light. Vast windows and surfaces in concrete-framed glass blocks allow sunlight to penetrate the building and enliven surfaces.

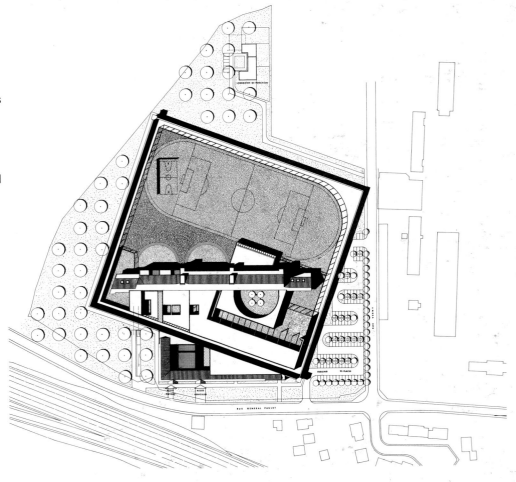

Site plan

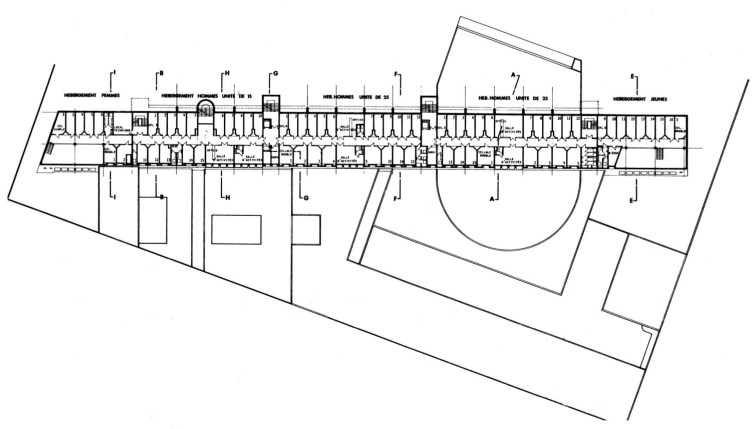

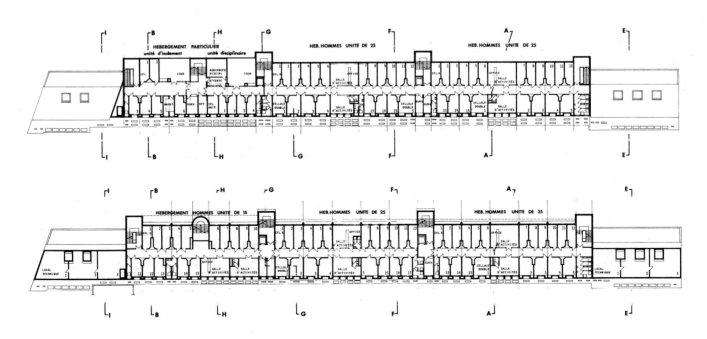

Fourth and third floor plans;
OPPOSITE: Second floor plan

PETER KULKA

SAXON STATE PARLIAMENT
Dresden, Germany

The architectural design of the most public building in the Free State of Saxony, the Saxon State Parliament, resolves both the meaning and image of the institution it houses. The basis of the design is the history of Dresden, its unmistakable typology and the peaceful revolution of 1989 which gave rise to the fresh rebirth of parliamentary democracy.

In spite of the appalling destruction in the Night of Bombs, February 1945, and the subsequent second wave of destruction in the years of socialist reconstruction that continued up to the present day, the city has very nearly preserved what the panoramic paintings of Canaletto so powerfully record: its unique and unmistakable skyline. This world famous 'cut-out silhouette' outlines the immediate surrounds of the new parliament and creates a symbiosis of city and landscape which has been compared with Florence.

The building commission, made up of representatives from all parliamentary parties, kept in step with the building process under the personal leadership of their chairman, Mr Erich Iltgen, and made well-informed and fast decisions without regard for party differences. The responsible institutions and authorities made decisions through personal contacts, avoiding pointless bureaucracy, and so were able to resolve any conflicts amicably and quickly. In this way, a creative atmosphere surrounded the work and the sense of urgency in the planning and building process left no opportunity for petty thoughts to arise.

In keeping with its context – low buildings along the Elbe, and higher domed buildings behind – the new building has a horizontal, rather than vertical, emphasis and takes its modest place close to the Elbe, in front of the old five-storey building with its 36-metre tower. This original building, an excellent example of new functionalism, was constructed in the 20s and is now a protected building under a strict programme of restoration.

The new parliament displays a clear architectural language, which owes much to modernism. It shows – like the other important buildings nearby – the self-confidence and uniqueness which are necessary for it to take its place in this exquisite architectural ensemble as a sign of our times. The transparent form of the new State Parliament completes the square made by Hollandische Strasse, Devrientstrasse, Kleine Packhofstrasse and Neue Terrasse, and together with the existing building it creates a taut interaction between the open and enclosed. The bright series of rooms, flooded with light which open out towards the river, permits the special functions of the parliament to move outwards and gives shape to the round, open assembly room as the architectural climax of the building; an expression of the parliamentary democracy now regained in this federal state.

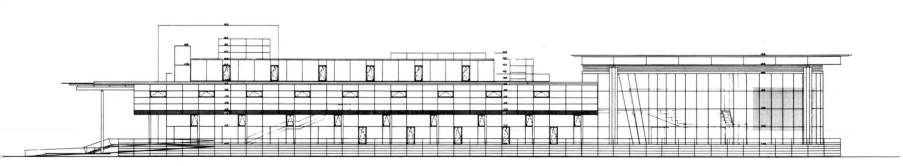

Riverside elevation of Debating Chamber

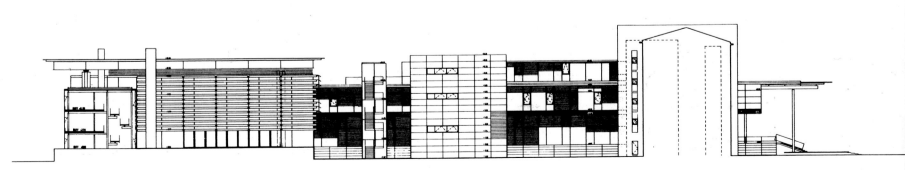

Court-side elevation of Debating Chamber

STAN ALLEN

DEMARCATING LINES
Beirut

Two projects, executed three years apart, for a city I have never seen: the first an invited proposal, exhibited in Beirut and the US shortly after the cease-fire, and before the process of reconstruction had begun; the second, an international competition sponsored by the development corporation which has already begun the process of rebuilding. Beirut is a place where the exercise of international power politics has practically destroyed the city; hence any architect working in Beirut is affected by complex relations of power, violence and space in the urban realm. In the course of developing the competition proposal, I was assisted by a student, in her early 20s, who had grown up in Beirut. I had expected her to be a source of local knowledge about the site, but it turned out that she had absolutely no memory of large areas of town because she had been denied access to this part of the city for 15 years of her life. The two projects are marked by distinct circumstances – the first a speculative proposal executed at a time when the future direction was still very fluid, and the second a highly specific response to a given site. These two projects also measure the distance my own thoughts have moved in the intervening years: from a more distanced commentary, to a programme of radical, involved pragmatism. As opposed to the open-ended speculation about the power of the architect in the city, in the first project, the more recent work takes a different line, proposing that the knowledge of the architect must be deployed in a direct and tactical manner, looking pragmatically for opportunities within the constraints of the existing power structure: working 'within the enemy's field of vision'

Demarcating Lines

'The souvenir', Walter Benjamin writes, 'is the relic secularised.' Travellers once made religious pilgrimages, a motivated journey to experience directly the presence of the relic. Today we travel as tourists to confirm an image we already possess. The image, as post-modern theory continually reminds us, precedes the reality. We bring home souvenirs to remind ourselves that we were there, even if there was no there there. 'In some ways the film is responsible for the destruction of the city. Through its dynamite of 1/24th of a second, it has produced hard won ruins through which we all become tourists.' (Benjamin) We can no longer sustain the difference between the experience of the traveller and the tourist. In the post-modern city all architects become tourists.

In 1991, I was asked to participate in an exhibition at Massachusetts Institute of Technology of proposals for the reconstruction of Beirut, which later travelled to the American University in Beirut. The city, at that time, was beginning to stabilise at the end of the civil war. Hashim Sarkis, a Lebanese archi-

tect, who had studied in this country, had proposed this exhibition and he had an interesting idea. He invited a number of architects who were either from or knew Beirut, and also a number of architects like myself who knew nothing about the city, and hence would have to deal with their limited knowledge of the place.

Beirut is a city which is in serious danger of disappearing. The scope of the destruction is difficult to imagine. However, one premise that the organisers asked us to consider was to call into question the simple opposition of construction/destruction. In this way we could begin to ask what latent structure was exposed by the destruction, and what new opportunities arose.

So in relationship to this problem there were three things which were important to me in working out the design of this project. The first was that given the extent and the violence of the conditions in Beirut, it seemed to me very important not to aestheticise the violence of the fragment. One had to find a way of working which did not treat the conditions of destruction as simply aesthetic material. The second, of course had to deal with making thematic my position as an outsider and thirdly, I had to deal with this condition that all of my knowledge of Beirut was mediated knowledge. That it was a kind of fiction, a kind of construction given to me through the sources of the news, media, maps, books and so on.
Stan Allen

OPPOSITE: Montages

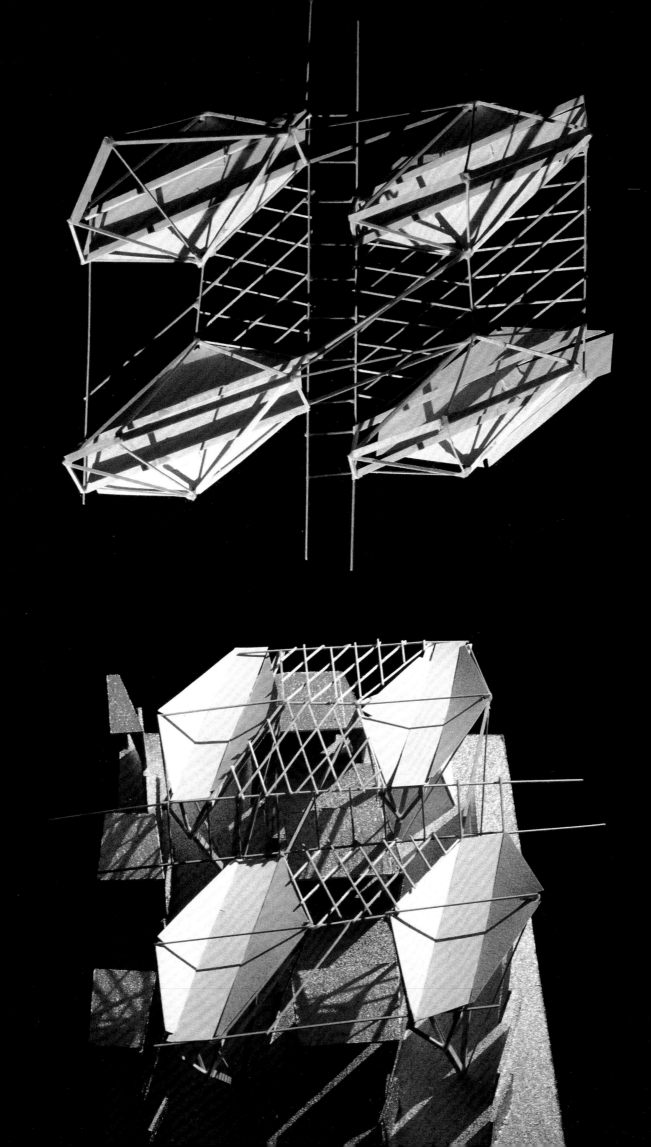

THE RECONSTRUCTION OF THE SOUKS
Beirut

When attempting to reconstruct a city which has grown slowly over time, encompassing the architectures of many cultures it is imperative to recognise the passage of time, and to accept the partial and incomplete nature of the planning process itself. Precise definition of the architecture is required, but it is also important to be aware of the intrinsic limits of the design operations. A city culture as complex as Beirut's cannot be recreated overnight on the basis of a single 'masterplan'. Therefore, it is essential to impose a measure of unity while respecting the essential diversity of the city to come. Towards this end we proposed four distinct but interrelated operations:
— To preserve and reconstruct as many of the existing historic structures as possible, accepting all of the limitations and irregularities that this might impose.
— To recover the ground of the site with a series of continuous surfaces, open in places, linking the upper and lower levels with stairs or ramps, and connecting the activities of the site with the context and the parking below. It should be noted here that the requirement to provide underground parking imposes a certain consistency to the site, dissolving the apparent separateness of individual buildings. This is a limitation we accepted as positive feature of the brief.
— To construct a series of new buildings to accommodate a variety of functions: markets, offices, residences, cinemas and department stores. Souks will be of lightweight construction, with louvred

sides for ventilation and protection.
— Finally and perhaps most importantly, a vast roof of steel and glass, extending throughout the site, stitches together a previously fragmented context. This roof provides protection from rain and sun, but is open on all sides. It creates a new horizon at a consistent height of 11 metres, covering the souks, the exhibition hall, restaurants and coffee houses as well as the fruit and vegetable market below. Supported on concrete piers (which carry up the module of the parking below), the glazing (about 60% of surface area) is carried on a steel superstructure. Additional sun protection is available in the form of lightweight awnings suspended below the structure.

Ours is a fundamentally architectural approach, concentrating the design effort at the level of the urban infrastructure. Unity is achieved by the continuous rhythm of the roof structure, while the diversity of city life is cultivated below. It should be noted here that while for the purposes of the competition, preliminary proposals are made for the souks and the other buildings, a major advantage of the scheme is that it anticipates the incorporation of various styles and designs within an overall framework. Hence it allows phasing, incremental realisation and broad participation in the reconstruction process. It is an optimistic approach, confident that the will to rebuild is strong enough to accommodate the complexity of the city to come.

Stan Allen

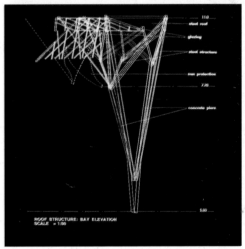

OPPOSITE: Structural model (study); FROM ABOVE: Second floor plan; roof structure

WOMEN AND CHILDREN'S CENTRE
Berlin

In order to feel empowered, a person must not feel marginalised by the society they inhabit. They need to feel they have the same opportunities, choices and rights as others, and that society's method of representing itself in language and aesthetics reflects rather than excludes them. This student project looks at how a building can be created for a group with particular needs who are being marginalised by society, and how the brief, the site, the process of design and the visual language can be worked together to provide a positive and empowering final piece.

The Brief
Whilst some East Germans gained individual freedoms with reunification, women with small children found themselves more restricted. Responsibilities previously considered social became their sole responsibility within the family. The starting point for this project was a desire to allow these women to participate equally in all levels of public life. To do this, a women's centre was to be provided, the first phase of which was to be a childcare centre, this having been narrowed down as the first step towards

giving them choices over the running of their lives, and to avoid having to make a mutually exclusive choice between career and family.

The Site
The site, between Potsdamer Platz and the Tiergarten occupies a position that until recently was neither East nor West Germany. Previously unusable by both sides, it is now in a central and important quarter in Berlin. This seemed an appropriate place for a marginalised group to make a statement to regain status.

The Process
It was crucial that the process by which the centre was created, and the language used should be one in which women are literate and articulate. The skills used should be those seen as being traditionally feminine in concern, and even control. This led to the use of fashion, or needlework, as the process for design. Thus, just as the Centre will try to make wider options available to women, so the process of design makes the creation of the building, and its final language, positive for women.

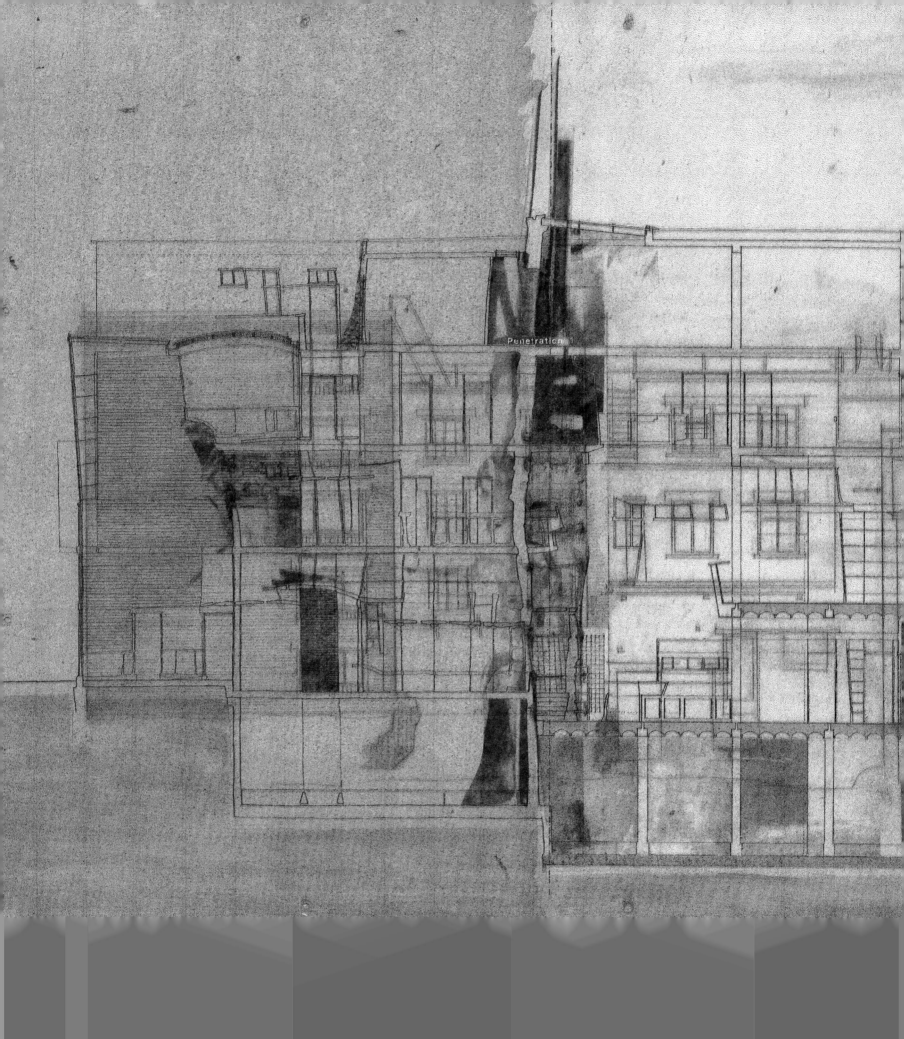

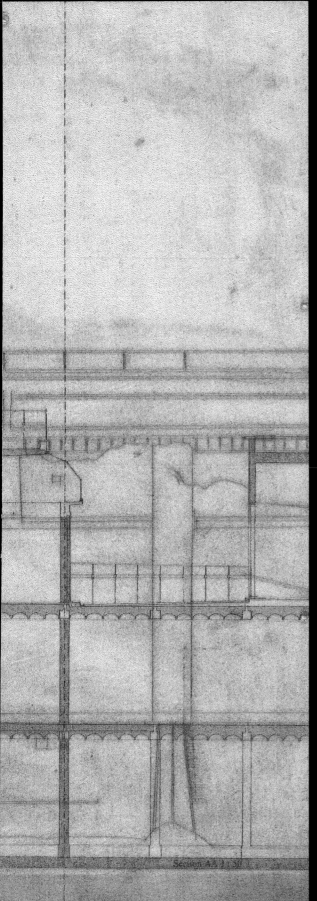

Section AA 1:50

SURROGACY CLINIC
London

The clinic(s), developed in this student project, investigate aspects of surrogacy, both 'informal' where there is the potential for minimum, or no medical intervention, and 'full' surrogacy where there is maximum medical intervention and the mother has no biological connection to the child she is nurturing. The intent is to expose and question how power structures are revealed and enforced within the notions of gender and childbirth within our culture. There is a crisis of definition where women are concerned, particularly in the realm of reproductive technology.

Issues of power are inextricably linked with desire and consequently notions of public and private. One has to consider these pertinent questions. Who controls who, what can be bought and sold, who makes the decisions, who has to live as a consequence of these decisions and is it every women's right to have a child?

Should a woman's egg become a commodity with an associated market value. Who determines the worth of a woman's egg? Is it down to one person and their judgement? Full surrogacy is largely dependent on male dominated medical science. Men have the power in the arts, sciences and literary fields because the categories of male and female, enforced by our culture which relegates women to the domestic sphere. We should attack and counter the hierarchical systems of value and power connected with the 'desire' to have a child and see what happens when traditional distinctions are eroded.

Architecture and its representation has the flexibility and potential for the displacement of existing dominant ideologies and the formulation of a new system of knowledge which confronts these issues.

The site – an existing structure – is considered as a metaphorical womb subject to external conditions both social and economic. It is within this speculative emptiness that the informal and full surrogacy clinics are inserted, or inseminated, and the perceived boundary between the two negotiated. This boundary becomes the main site of manipulation. In fact, the existing fabric of the building can be considered as a surrogate body, or womb, provided to accommodate the intended insertion.

In the context of this project, the domestic becomes a metaphor for self-help surrogacy and the commercial a metaphor for full surrogacy. The link between the new insertion(s) and the existing is a metaphor for the dependent loaded relationship between surrogate mother and child

OPPOSITE: Section; OVERLEAF: Insemination or insertion into existing building

Surrogacy clinic (s) Farringdon

Informal self help   Full

area of separation manipulation

Expansion joint

Insemination: Insertion into existing building